SEASONS
OF
LIFE

The 1997 Methodist Companion

Seasons of Life
© Methodist Publishing House, 1996

Illustrations © Steven Hall

Printed in Great Britain by Clays Ltd, St Ives plc

ISBN 1 85852 073 8

CONTENTS

FOREWORD

I find that the parts of the newspapers that I go for straightaway or, if I'm pressed, save up for that quiet moment later on, are the articles headed 'A day in the life of . . .' or 'My childhood . . .' They are often at the back of the supplement. Alternatively, the 'profiles' will often catch my eye. There's nothing so interesting as reading about people; finding that little scrap of information, often completely unexpected, which makes you feel that you know this person.

If you are like me, then this book, *Seasons of Life* is your kind of book. In it you will discover what Leslie Griffiths didn't do until he was sixteen and what Bruce Kent did do only just a few years ago. You will find out what Bernard Weatherill's 'Five Rs' are and where Pauline Webb longs to be, and much, much more besides.

But more importantly you will be able to share in how a group of completely different people reflect on their experiences of life in its varied seasons. Again, if you are like me, you will catch yourself reading with a knowing smile or perhaps a tiny tear at the corner of an eye. For these people are writing with integrity and they are writing about human life, theirs, yours, mine.

Seasons of Life will also stir the memory. As I read Lord Soper on Proust and 'Times Remembered', I recalled an ordination service in a Durham mining community a dozen and a half years ago and Donald Soper telling the ordinands, after Proust: 'Remember this day, especially in the testing times. Remember the day you were ordained.' I wonder if any of those ordinands are reading this book now.

In the natural world, the world of sowing and reaping, generally speaking the fruit comes in summer or early autumn. The interesting thing about the human seasons is that you can go to any season and find fruit; in the boy Samuel and in the aged Anna alike.

That is the mystery and the glory of human life.

This is a lovely book, interlaced with prayers and quotations from a myriad sources. You will find fruits of all kinds and in all seasons. Enjoy it!

Nigel Collinson

For you, O Lord, are my hope, my trust, O Lord, from my youth. Upon you have I leaned from my birth; it was you who took me from my mother's womb.

Psalm 71: 5-6

SPRING

Just Outside the Camp

Leslie Griffiths

For the first ten years of my life my whole world consisted of five streets of terraced houses interspersed with a handful of council semi-detacheds. Glanmor, Silver, Morlan, Woodbrook and Burrows terraces made up the oldest part of the Carmarthenshire village of Burry Port. From the moment the Great Western Railway pushed its way from London to Fishguard, our old bit of the town became isolated from the newer parts that sprang up from the mid-nineteenth century. So we were something of a ghetto, surrounded not only by the main line but by acres of railway sidings, a power station, railway sheds, smelting factories and, *pièce de résistance*, a sewage farm.

I was born in No 25 Glanmor Terrace but, through the breakup of my parents' marriage and the state of the law at that time, my mother and her two boys were kicked out of the family home with just one week's notice. We ended up living in a lean-to room on a builder's yard just outside the five street ghetto where I was born. Just outside. I sometimes feel I've lived the whole of my life just outside the camp. But, for all that, I joined in the street-life which saw our gang out in the fields fighting other gangs from different parts of the town. We fought either with stones or fists. It was a rough-and-ready life. One of my early neighbours was given a life sentence for murder. Every Saturday night there were fights on the streets when the pub closed its doors. There were few comforts for any of us.

My mother went out to work to keep body and soul together. Burry Port was at the heart of the tinplate industry which supplied ninety-five per cent of Britain's output at this time. Sometimes my mother forgot to take her lunch to work, and, when that happened, it was my job to take it (in one of those old-fashioned Oxo boxes) down to the tin-works at lunchtime. I remember seeing her at work. She had to carry a pile of steel sheets to a rolling mill. There she had to feed the sheets one at a time through the mill – it looked rather like a clothes mangle – where the next person in the process caught them before carrying them on to the pickling baths. It was work fit only for animals and it didn't take long to break my mother's body. She barely survived serious surgery in 1952. I was ten at the time, my brother nine.

Food was scarce. I didn't eat meat at home (except at Christmas) until I was sixteen. I'm now (as are most people who've been poor) a determined meat eater. New clothes were even more difficult to come by. I never wore underwear or pyjamas until I went to university. My brother and I had three pairs of socks between us, one each to wear with the third in the wash. The winters were particularly hard. We couldn't afford to buy enough fuel, so we went out, buckets and sacks in hand, to gather in wood and cinders from the engine sheds. And there were times too when desperation drove us to the coal wagons down from the Gwendraeth valley. They left Burry Port a little lighter than they'd arrived!

At some time in this whole sorry business we became candidates for help from the National Assistance Board. The Welfare State held us together and this experience has made me one of its fiercest defenders. But those who dispensed its benefits could sometimes be impossibly patronising and insultingly overbearing. I was about ten years of age when I physically removed one such person from our house because he was speaking to my mother as if she had brought her poverty on herself and was the cause of her children's misery. Since then I've always had a short fuse with officious people who've little intelligence in their heads and less humanity in their hearts but who, because they are on the other side of the counter, hold their suppliants to ransom and belittle them. If you want to see me lose my rag, just produce one such bumptiously bourgeois petty official for me!

There was just one chapel in our little community. It was Wesleyan Methodist and had been built in 1866 for the Cornish miners who'd come over to work in the metal-smelting factories. It's likely that Hugh Price Hughes, living in Carmarthen and at that time a theological student at Richmond College, was present for the opening, a strange coincidence in view of the fact that I was to succeed him as superintendent of the West London Mission which he founded in 1887 (I didn't follow him until 1986!). My mother, who'd attended a Baptist chapel in her youth, had long since given up attending worship. But, to give herself a little peace and quiet on a Sunday afternoon, she sent the two of us to Sunday school at the chapel. And that's how I became a Methodist. I've since travelled to the far corners of the earth and sat at the feet of some of the

6

finest teachers of my generation. But I've never learned anything more profound than I did from that bunch of working class saints in long ago Burry Port.

Each of them could be described as 'Christianity on two legs'; they were living examples of the power of God's love to change lives. They didn't need to bark like dogs or speak in tongues. Their language was action, their prayer love, and the Spirit manifested itself by turning a couple of dozen rough-and-ready people into a veritable army with a combined strength far greater than the sum of their individual parts. From them I learned the absolute priority of love over every other single aspect of Christian living, over doctrine and discipline alike. These people saw to it that my mother's poverty would not deprive her children of the necessities of life. I can't possibly count the number of times a garment, a school outing, some food, a Christmas present, magically arrived at exactly the right moment it needed to. The people of Israel were given manna and quails. Our provision was more varied but just as heaven sent.

I passed the eleven plus examination and entered an entirely new world. The number fifteen bus took me to the Llanelli Grammar School and a world of bank managers' sons (or so it seemed to me at the time). They spoke posh and dressed smoothly. I made good friends and was frequently invited to their homes. But it was impossible to invite my friends home. I remember how proud we all were when (I must have been about fifteen) we bought a roll of lino at the Co-op and covered the floor of our room for the first time. It served as kitchen, living room and bathroom for many years, and for a short while it was a bedroom too. Every Friday evening my mother and brother would go out so that I could have my bath. The galvanised tin bath (in which the clothes had been washed earlier in the week) was filled with water from a bucket on the open stove. Later that evening it was my turn to go out so that the others could take to the waters.

Holding all this together was my mother. She was an extraordinary woman. She left school at fourteen and went into service in Ilfracombe, scrubbing floors and serving as a chambermaid. Her unhappy marriage brought her little joy and she resolved to take no further risks in this area until her sons were independent of her. She smoked Loadstone cigarettes (there were twelve in a packet, I remember) and filled in a Vernons pools coupon every week. Just now and again she'd put sixpence each way on a horse. These were not extravagances. They were the only pleasures in her bitterly hard life. Let the one that is without sin cast the first stone. She was a dedicated mother. Many times I remember my brother and myself eating when there wasn't enough for her. And yet, every Sunday, we'd see Mrs Reidy (a Roman Catholic widow who lived round the corner) at our table for tea. The fare was always bread and butter and jam followed by rice pudding.

After I'd gone to the Grammar School, my mother would willingly hold my Latin primer and listen to me recite my vocabulary homework. She didn't have a clue what it was all about but she did her best to help me cope. Not once did she ask me to leave school to

8

take a job when I knew that that would solve the family budgeting problems 'at a stroke'. She remains the clearest evidence of just how wrong those who castigate and stigmatise single mothers can be.

I passed my A level exams in 1960 (B-grade in English and French, C in Latin) and gained entry to the University at Cardiff. My mother and some of the chapel saints came to the station to see me off. The only capital reserves I had were a Sunday school faith and a happy childhood. I was to find out how many of my contemporaries, despite being better off financially, had far less than I. For the whole of my eighteen and a half years, I'd never spent a single night away from home. No holidays, no weekends with friends, nothing. For the fifteen years I'd been at school, I'd never missed a single day through illness. Mine had been a remarkably stable childhood despite all the hardship. But now, as I saw my mother barely able to restrain her tears, I knew that my childhood was over. We said our goodbyes and I promised to be good and to write. When I got my last glimpse of my mother, some of the saints were consoling her and helping her home. I cried like a baby all the way to Cardiff.

If a child lives with criticism
He learns to condemn;
If a child lives with hostility
He learns to fight;
If a child lives with ridicule
He learns to be shy;
If a child lives with shame
He learns to be guilty.

If a child lives with tolerance
He learns to be patient;
If a child lives with encouragement
He learns confidence;
If a child lives with praise
He learns to appreciate;
If a child lives with fairness
He learns justice.

If a child lives with security
He learns faith;
If a child lives with approval
He learns to like himself;
If a child lives with acceptance
*   and friendship*
He learns to give love to the world.

Anonymous

March 22nd: On the 27th of February 1788, Stone-curlews were heard to pipe; and on March 1st, after it was dark some were passing over the village, as might be perceived by their quick, short note, which they use in their nocturnal excursions by way of watch-word, that they may stray, and lose their companions. Thus we see, that retire whithersoever they may in the winter, they return again early in the spring, and are, as it now appears, the first summer birds that come back . . . Perhaps the mildness of the season may have quickened the emigration of the curlews this year.

Gilbert White, *Journals*

Susanna was certainly the principal factor in the upbringing of both John and Charles. Her husband remained very much in the background, for reasons of both temperament and circumstance. Susanna's methods were, by modern standards, unduly severe: she was not averse from the use of the rod as a means of discipline, the children were to be seen and not heard at mealtimes, and even the babies were not allowed to cry, except very softly. Formal education began when the age of five was reached, and lasted for six hours a day from the start . . .

When John Wesley came to found schools of his own, he looked back to the educational principles and practice of his mother for guidance.

Rupert E. Davies, *Methodism*

11

When I was a boy, there was but one permanent ambition among my comrades in our village on the west bank of the Mississippi River. That was, to be a steam boatman. We had transient ambitions of other sorts, but they were only transient. When a circus came and went, it left us all burning to become clowns; the first black minstrel show that came to our section left us all suffering to try that kind of life; now and then we had a hope that if we lived and were good, God would permit us to be pirates. These ambitions faded out, each in its turn; but the ambition to be a steam boatman always remained . . . By and by one of our boys went away. He was not heard of for a long time. At last he turned up as apprentice engineer or 'striker' on a steam boat. This thing shook the bottom out of all my Sunday-school teachings. That boy had been notoriously worldly, and I just the reverse; yet he was exalted to this eminence, and I left in obscurity and misery.

Mark Twain

The great man is he who does not lose his child's heart.

Mencius

12

Fair Daffodils, we weep to see
You haste away so soon;
As yet the early-rising sun
Has not attained his noon.
Stay, stay
Until the hasting day
Has run
But to the evensong;
And, having prayed together; we
Will go with you along
We have short time to stay, as you
We have as short a spring;
As quick a growth to meet decay
As you, or anything
We die
As your hours do, and dry
Away
Like to the summer's rain;
Or as the pearls of morning's dew,
Ne'er to be found again.

Robert Herrick

Every child comes into the world with the message that God does not despair of man.

Rabindranath Tagore

The Chapel in the Valley

Hazel Bradley

I had hardly slept a wink, and so at ten to nine when my father called me down to breakfast, I was already out of bed and pulling my dressing-gown around my shoulders. Mum was up, too, finding some clothes for my younger sister, but I sensed her mind was elsewhere as she sorted through the drawer, her eyes glancing at the mantelpiece clock every few seconds. The hour was striking and I could hear the voice of the announcer reading the news on the wireless. It was louder than usual; someone had turned up the volume. The bowl of cornflakes in front of me had begun to go soggy as I fidgeted about on my chair, not at all inclined to allow anything into the mass of fluttering butterflies that seemed to be inhabiting my stomach.

All eyes were now on the clock and as the bulletin finished at two minutes past nine and the familiar music of the next programme started, my whole family sat silently round the table like some sort of Madame Tussaud's display.

I had only just had my twelfth birthday. For a child like me from a very ordinary Croydon home in 1960, it was going to be an extraordinary experience to hear my voice singing out from the wireless, especially in a programme to which I'd listened every Sunday morning of my life.

Sandy Macpherson's 'Chapel in the Valley' had been on the air since just after the Second World War and had a huge audience. It portrayed a country chapel whose members enjoyed a traditional service with well-loved hymns, and, of course, good organ playing. Sandy introduced the characters taking part; a baritone from the choir who would be heard practising the hymns and sacred songs for the morning service, the organist running through the voluntary and a little girl from the Sunday school who would try out the pieces especially chosen for the young people.

For ten years I had the privilege to play that little girl and as I now look back to a season of childhood rich in happy experiences and wonderful people, I can see the foundation on which the rest of my life has been built.

I thought Sandy to be quite the gentlest giant I had ever met. Standing well over six feet tall and with a name that was known in every household, he could easily have appeared intimidating to one rather small for her twelve years. Instead, on our very first meeting, he crouched down until our heads were level and only then did he introduce himself to me, nearly toppling over in the process. The ice was broken and in that moment I knew that I had met an adult with whom I could feel at ease. During the next ten years we travelled many miles together, making appearances all over the country in concerts and recitals. Most of the journeys were by train which gave us plenty of opportunity to share ideas and just enjoy each other's company. The different generations have so much to learn from each other and I am sure that those conversations and the relationship that blossomed over the years helped me to understand that. Perhaps that's why I'm always drawn to organisations like our church drama group, that encourages members from eight to eighty to work and play together.

When we arrived at our destination, usually a church needing to raise some money, Sandy would book into a nearby hotel, and I was always billeted out with one of the church families. As a result I have friends all over the country. It was a little daunting to be the guest of total strangers, but everyone was so kind and when in later years I too was given a hotel room, I missed the warmth and friendliness of a family home. I loved meeting new people and when each year the list of venues was sent out to me for the autumn and spring seasons, I would immediately run for the atlas to find out where I would be going. It was sometimes hard to fit in my school work with an ever demanding schedule of recordings and concerts but somehow most of it got done. However, I would be the first to admit that a bunk on the London to Durham sleeper train was never an ideal environment for attempting maths problems!

My parents were, and still are, great believers in both working and playing hard and I have always encouraged my own children to enjoy a variety of activities. Of course, to strive for academic excellence is always worthwhile, but surely not at the expense of everything else that is good in life. I am sure that if I had concentrated solely on my A level study I could have achieved higher grades but the social skills I developed during that period could never have been learned inside a classroom and yet have served me for a lifetime.

Today people often comment on my confident manner in front of an audience whether it be 'live' or through the medium of radio. It has not always been so. I can remember when I was fourteen waiting in the wings of the Odeon in Llandudno and shaking so much that the bows on my dress were jiggling around like butterflies under the influence of too much nectar! As I started the long walk to the centre of the stage, the spotlight picked me up and at the same time made the audience disappear from my sight. It was absolutely terrifying. I was so afraid of forgetting the words of my songs, and yet in reality they were so etched into my subconscious that all these years later I can rattle off the words of pieces like 'At the end of the day' and 'It is no secret' without a second thought. Nerves can still be a problem, but the prayer that I said as a child just before I went on, is one I still use today:

> O God, I know it's natural to be nervous, but please, don't let me look it!

The first hymn that I sang on 'Chapel in the Valley' was 'I love to hear the story that angel voices tell', by Emily Miller. I have never worked out how many children's hymns I sang in total for those broadcasts, but most came from *The Sunday School Hymnary* or *Child Songs*. I used to practise them at home with my aunt playing the piano and my mother coaching me on how to express the words: 'If they can't understand what you're singing about then there's no point in singing at all.'

I was encouraged to look at what the hymnwriter was trying to say and it is something that I have continued to do ever since. Al Cohn, writing in the New York Times, said, 'It's what you listen to when you are growing up that you always come back to.' When I look back now at some of the words I used to sing I cringe, as they belong to an era long gone, but all spoke of the love of God for children, and from a very early age I felt that love surrounding me all the time. Later I wanted to share the good news with all those listening. I still believe that hymn singing is one of the most satisfying ways of worshipping God. Nothing we do is adequate but some might say that a thousand voices joining together in 'Love Divine' comes as near as we're going to get!

I had a very special childhood to which I look back with immense pleasure, not in some nostalgic, sentimental way but as the beginning of my journey through life. A time of learning, of feeling, of challenging, watched over by loving parents and a caring church.

There was no actual 'Chapel in the Valley', although many wrote in for the address. It existed only in the imaginative minds of Sandy Macpherson and the loyal Sunday morning listeners, but the wealth and variety of opportunity it gave to this child of the Sixties was a reality, and one that has echoed again and again throughout all the seasons of my life.

O Lord Jesus Christ, we pray thee to pour thy Spirit upon the students of all nations; that they may consecrate themselves to thy service, and may come to love and understand one another through their common obedience to thee.

Anonymous

I suppose I had a normal middle-class upbringing. The only loss was I never saw my father until I was seven because he was in India and my mother either had to be with him or with us. The First World War was on so he couldn't get home till I was seven. I was sent off to boarding school at seven so I really saw very little of my parents. My mother died when I was seventeen. Looking back, I think that was a great loss, but otherwise it was a very comfortable life.

I went to Lancing, which is a church school, and there were many people there who had a big influence on me. The whole atmosphere of the place was very much dominated by the chapel, one of the great buildings of England; it suited me. I don't think in those days there was any sense of rebelliousness about having to go to chapel twice a day as we did, and on Sundays; it was taken for granted. Lancing was a very progressive public school; the relationship between boys and masters was very good. And to one or two of those masters I owe an enormous amount; they certainly had a great influence on me.

Bishop Trevor Huddleston

I remember, I remember
  The house where I was born,
The little window where the sun
  Came peeping in at morn;
He never came a wink too soon
  Nor brought too long a day;
But now, I often wish the night
  Had borne my breath away.

I remember, I remember
  The roses, red and white,
The violets, and the lily-cups —
  Those flowers made of light!
The lilacs where the robin built,
  And where my brother set
The laburnum on his birthday —
  The tree is living yet!

I remember, I remember
  Where I was used to swing,
And thought the air must rush as fresh
  To swallows on the wing;
My spirit flew in feathers then
  That is so heavy now,
And summer pools could hardly cool
  The fever on my brow.

I remember, I remember,
  The fir trees dark and high;
I used to think their slender tops
  Were close against the sky:
It was a childish ignorance,
  But now 'tis little joy
To know I'm farther off from heaven
  Than when I was a boy.

                    Thomas Hood

It is mind that you have to draw out, and mould, and fit for its duties to itself, to mankind and to its Maker. From the child's first entrance into your school, your object is to train him to think, and to teach him how to think.

John Scott,
19th century Methodist educationalist

Never tell a young person that something cannot be done. God may have been waiting for countless centuries for somebody ignorant of the impossibility to do that thing.

Anonymous

Young people set their watches, for right time or wrong, by the watches of their elders.

Anonymous

Youth supposes; age knows.

Welsh proverb

X

Youth is not a time of life . . . it is a state of mind.
Nobody grows old by merely living a number of years;
people grow old only by deserting their ideals.
Years wrinkle the skin, but to give up enthusiasm
wrinkles the soul.
Worry, doubt, self-distrust, fear and despair . . .
these are the long, long years that bow the head and
turn the growing spirit back to dust.
Whether seventy or sixteen, there is in every being's
heart the love of wonder, the sweet amazement at the
stars and the starlike things and thoughts, the
undaunted challenge of events, the unfailing childlike
appetite for what next,
and the joy of the game of life.
You are as young as your faith, as old as your doubt;
as young as your self-confidence, as old as your fear;
as young as your hope, as old as your despair.

X

Anonymous

Round the camp-fires they still remember an old
Indian who used to listen to the boasts of the young
braves rejoicing in their youth, and presently would
say with a smile: 'But the sixties have all the twenties
and forties in them.'

Anonymous

A Child's-eye View of the World

John Newton

Denis Healey is surely one of the most well-read of British politicians. In both his autobiography, *The Time of My Life*, and his anthology, *My Secret Planet*, he shares the fruits of his wide reading. One of his favourite authors is Thomas Traherne, the seventeenth-century Anglican poet and mystic. Lord Healey is drawn to Traherne not only by the poet's incomparable use of English, but also by his love of children.

It is notoriously difficult for an adult writer to recapture the child's eyeview of the world. Thomas Traherne, in his classic *Centuries of Meditations*, seems to Denis Healey – and to me – to have come nearer to it than most. In his own inimitable style, he paints for us a picture of the world as it appeared, in all its breathtaking wonder, to himself as a young child:

> The corn was orient and immortal wheat, which never should be reaped, nor was ever sown. I thought it had stood from everlasting to everlasting. The dust and stones of the street were as precious as gold: the gates were at first the end of the world. The green trees when I saw them first through one of the gates transported and ravished me, their sweetness and unusual beauty made my heart to leap, and almost mad with ecstasy, they were such strange and wonderful things. The Men! O

what venerable and reverend creatures did the aged seem! Immortal Cherubims! And young men glittering and sparkling Angels, and maids strange seraphic pieces of life and beauty! Boys and girls tumbling in the street, and playing, were moving jewels. I knew not that they were born or should die; But all things abided eternally as they were in their proper places. Eternity was manifest in the Light of the Day, and something infinite behind everything appeared: which talked with my expectation X and moved my desire . . .

The whole picture is shot through with light. His words speak of brightness – 'orient', 'gold', 'glittering and sparkling', 'moving jewels'. It is one of the charming touches in Denis Healey's own appreciation of Traherne that, as he reads and quotes him, he sees from his study window some small children playing down below, and at once sees them as two of the 'moving jewels' of whom Traherne writes.

The sadness is, of course, as Traherne himself admits, that it doesn't last. The vision fades into the common light of day. Traherne concludes this passage of his *Meditations* thus:

ᴸ The skies were mine, and so were the sun and moon and stars, and all the World was mine; and I the only spectator and enjoyer of it . . . So that with much ado I was corrupted, and made to learn the dirty devices of this world. Which now I unlearn, and become, as it were, a little child again that I may enter into the Kingdom of God . . .

Reading Traherne, you begin to understand what G. K. Chesterton meant when he called childhood a magnificent failed experiment in living. Wordsworth understood it all too well, when he reflected on the way in which 'Shades of the prison house begin to close about the growing boy', and the glory of childhood's dawn 'Fades into the light of common day'. Yet Wordsworth, as a poet and a Christian, also knew that it was possible to renew the sense of wonder as an adult. There could be no going back to childhood: a flaming sword barred the access to that lost paradise. And yet the experience of the glory of the world as God's creation could be reborn in the mature man or woman.

Wordsworth himself cherished that experience, as he makes clear in his miniature poem on the rainbow:

> My heart leaps up when I behold
> A rainbow in the sky;
> So was it when my life began;
> So is it now I am a man;
> So be it when I shall grow old,
> Or let me die.

All of which points us to the characteristic words of Jesus about that attitude of heart and mind which is called for if we would enter the kingdom:

> At that time the disciples came to Jesus and asked, 'Who is the greatest in the kingdom of heaven?' He called a child, whom he put among them, and said, 'Truly, I tell you, unless you change and become like children, you will never enter the kingdom of heaven. Whoever

25

> becomes humble like this child is the greatest in
> the kingdom of heaven.
>
> (Matthew18:1-4 NRSV)

But the change and the becoming are hard. Indeed, they are only possible by the transforming power of grace. Nicodemus' haunting question speaks for us all, 'But how can someone be born when he is old? . . . Can he enter his mother's womb a second time and be born?' It's a question that has built into it the answer No. But what is humanly impossible is not beyond the grace of God. Jesus answered, 'In very truth I tell you, no one can enter the kingdom of God without being born from water and spirit . . . You ought not to be astonished when I say, "You must all be born again." ' (John 3:4-7 REB).

Charles Wesley takes up this theme of the childlike heart which enters the kingdom, and extemporises upon it in the light of the Gospel:

> Lord, that I may learn of thee,
> Give me true simplicity;
> Wean my soul, and keep it low,
> Willing thee alone to know.
>
> * * * *
>
> Of my boasted wisdom spoiled,
> Docile, helpless, as a child,
> Only seeing in thy light,
> Only walking in thy might.
>
> (HP737)

And if we are brought to 'seeing in thy light', then for us, as for Traherne, 'Eternity' may again be 'manifest in the light of day'.

Yes, God is good — in earth and sky,
   From ocean depths and spreading wood,
Ten thousand voices seem to cry:
   God made us all, and God is good.

The sun that keeps his trackless way,
   And downward pours his golden flood,
Night's sparkling hosts, all seem to say
   In accents clear, that God is good.

The merry birds prolong the strain,
   Their song with every spring renewed;
And balmy air, and falling rain.
   Each softly whispers: God is good.

I hear it in the rushing breeze;
   The hills that have for ages stood,
The echoing sky and roaring seas,
   All swell the chorus: God is good.

Yes, God is good, all nature says,
   By God's own hand with speech endued;
And man, in louder notes of praise,
   Should sing for joy that God is good.

For all thy gifts we bless thee, Lord,
   But chiefly for our heavenly food;
Thy pardoning grace, thy quickening word,
   These prompt our song, that God is good.

                    John Hampden Gurney

The son of Pietro Bernadone, a cloth merchant, there was little in Francis' youth to hint at what was to come. As a young man, when not helping his father, he enjoyed a life of song and revelry with like-minded youths of the town. His conversion came slowly after a series of adventures and misadventures and culminated as Francis was praying in the little ruined church of St Damien. There he heard God say to him, 'Francis, rebuild my church.' Taking it literally, Francis began to rebuild the walls of the chapel with his own hands.

Avery Brooke

An adolescent is independent enough to create his or her own world instead of the jaded and compromised values and attitudes of the older generation. Youth is a phase of unsullied idealism, though every young person quickly discovers life is not that simple. Independence means not only a distancing from childhood and parents, but also from peers. Individuality becomes the principle item on each young person's agenda. He or she discovers, 'I am unique.' A self-image comes into clear focus, if a little anxiously . . . What now of parents and other authority figures? Adolescents are ambivalent. On the one hand they want to reject them. So they form a counter-culture, focused around youthful idols (pop stars, footballers) and expressed in fashions which are designed to offend or irritate the older generation. On the other hand young people want to respect their elders if the latter consistently adhere to their own values and authority structures because they are believed to be life-enhancing.

David Deeks,
Pastoral Theology: An Inquiry

My dear Father,
I think I ought to be a Wesleyan Minister,
Your affectionate son.

My dear Boy,
I would rather that you should be a Wesleyan Minister
than Lord Chancellor,
Your affectionate Father.

Correspondence between
Revd Hugh Price Hughes
and his father

*As a youngster I had always felt a profound sense of vocation. If it
had been possible for women to be ordained to the ministry, I don't
think there is any doubt that I would have sought ordination as a
student. I remember once asking one of the elder statesmen of the
church on his visit to the university what room there was in
Methodism for a woman theologian. He said, 'Well, none.'*

Frances Young

Blessed be childhood, which brings down something of
heaven into the midst of our rough earthliness.

Henri Frederic Amiel

The few mashed potatoes left in the bowl are beginning to form a yellowish crust, and tiny pearls of grease float on the water that once covered green beans. Napkins, plates and silverware lay strewn across the table that, not long before, someone's hands had placed in order for a festive meal.

Young voices whisper at one corner of the table. Finally, one speaks aloud, 'Gram, tell us again about when you were a girl.' They have all heard the story before many times. Yet the satisfaction that comes from hearing their grandmother's voice speaking those familiar words is like sharing the most special of secrets. The voice of the teller, warm and quiet, begins, 'I remember . . .'

The telling of stories is woven into the fabric of our lives. When we speak about the deepest hurts and joys of ourselves and our families, we break into story. The stories we heard growing up – from the Bible, from the Brothers Grimm, from our parents or neighbours or friends – shape our images of who we are in the world and of the communities of which we are a part.

Michael E. Williams,
Voices from Unseen Rooms:
Storytelling and Community

So Abram rose, and clave the wood, and went,
And took the fire with him, and a knife.
And as they journeyed both of them together,
Isaac the first-born spake and said, My Father,
Behold the preparations, fire and iron,
But where the lamb for this burnt-offering?
Then Abram bound the youth with belts and straps,
And builded parapets and trenches there,
And stretched forth the knife to slay his son.
When lo! an angel called him out of heaven,
Saying, Lay not thy hand upon the lad,
Neither do anything to him. Behold,
A ram, caught in a thicket by its horns;
Offer the Ram of Pride instead of him.
But the old man would not so, but slew his son —
And half the seed of Europe, one by one.

Wilfred Owen,
The Parable of the
Old Men and the Young

The world is passing through troubled times. The young people of today think of nothing but themselves. They have no reverence for parents or old age; they are impatient of all restraint; they talk as if they alone knew everything, and what passes for wisdom with us is foolishness with them. As for the girls, they are foolish and immodest and unwomanly in speech, behaviour and dress.

Peter the Hermit, 1274

Childhood Conversations

David Coffey

Once upon a time I was a child. I played and thought as a child and on the journey to adulthood I discovered a love for books, music and sport. But where on this journey did I receive what children most deserve? What Jonathan Sachs memorably terms 'a map of meaning by which to chart a way through a confusing and chaotic world'. I have come to the conclusion that my 'map of meaning' was written in the lives of dozens of people who offered me visible evidence of the Christian faith.

Someone has said that we need five Gospels to nurture us in the Christian way: Matthew, Mark, Luke and John, and the fifth gospel which is the attractive life-style of a disciple of Jesus Christ.

Oliver Goldsmith's village preacher was a powerful influence on those who heard him preach:

Even children followed with endearing wile, and plucked his gown, to share the good man's smile.

Geoffrey Chaucer's parson was renowned for first following the word before he taught it:

His business was to show a fair behaviour and draw men thus to Heaven and their Saviour.

R S Thomas' country clergy left no books:

> Rather they wrote on men's hearts and in the minds
> of young children sublime words
> Too soon forgotten.

I have reflected on the people in my childhood days who wrote sublime words in my mind.

I have in writing the charitable words of the examiner for my grade one pianoforte exam. He had to include in his notes that I had fallen off the piano stool during one of the pieces and managed to mask the drama of the moment with notable discretion: 'This piece was good and had vitality, in spite of one slight stumble.'

Less notable was the cautionary counsel of a stern and forbidding Aunt who wrote in my autograph book when I was eight years of age: 'It shows a fine command of language to say nothing.' Which may have been sound advice for a lively nephew but revealed little insight into my future needs as a preacher!

Or imagine the plight of seven-year-old having to defend the stabbing insights of a form teacher, who had written in one of my earliest end-of-year school reports: 'David has ability, and should do well when he has learned obedience and self-control.' It did not improve the situation with my parents when, a year later, the end of term report concluded with the memorable remark: 'We wish David every success on the games field.'

These were momentary events on the journey to maturity. More importantly there were the conversations I enjoyed. One writer has said that our nurture and incorporation into the Christian way requires 'not a one-time meeting, but an ongoing conversation', conversations which enable children to develop a little at a time at their own pace and draw them into a living faith in Christ.

Apart from the considerable influence of my parents, to whom I owe so much, my late grandmother remains an outstanding example of an adult who could hold such ongoing conversations with a child.

At the beginning of this century my grandparents had emigrated from Northern Ireland to Consett, County Durham. Until 1840 Consett Hill was a hamlet of thatched cottages and then came the Consett Iron Company, described at the Great Exhibition of 1851 as 'the largest in the kingdom'. By the end of the nineteenth century, Consett was producing a tenth of the nation's steel output. The steel owners brought in Irish workers to strengthen the workforce, but this resulted in uneasy community relations, culminating in the infamous Battle of the Blue Heaps riot when English and Irish workers had to be separated by soldiers. My grandfather was an Irish foreman at the Iron Company.

My grandparents had nine children and my mother was their fifth child. Most of my uncles and aunts lived with their families in the Consett region. My mother had removed to London for nursing training and after she had married my father, they began their family life first in Purley, Surrey and later in Bournemouth. As early as six years of age I was travelling from Bournemouth to Consett to spend part of my summer holidays with my grandmother. My grandfather had died before I was born.

I loved spending holidays with my grandmother in the mining village of Hamsterley. Perhaps it was the Irish background that enabled my grandmother to give a small boy permission to eat his pudding before his main meal and enjoy fruitcake on the breakfast table. She lived to within six months of her hundredth birthday and when she was in her nineties, suffering from another broken limb from which she would eventually recover, the local doctor reputedly told her: 'Mrs Willis, you are so healthy you will never die, we will have to shoot you!'

I remember most of all in our ongoing conversations the way she would impress a truth upon the mind with a memorable aphorism. Her standard phrase for an ethical dilemma was, 'Always ask the question, what would Jesus do?' Her epigram for coping with the mystery of God's providence was simply expressed in three words: 'It will pass.' This was not a stoic endurance because she would normally expand on the phrase by saying that we should always take the long view. 'Give God time,' she would say, 'he needs time to bring things to pass.' Her doctrine of God led her to believe that he was actively working for the good of those who love him and we must never judge a human situation prematurely. Give God time to work out his good purposes.

Many years later, when I had become a Christian and was facing some of the challenging situations of life, I would be reminded of my grandmother's teaching. We cannot always understand what God is doing. We are not told he is working to make life comfortable for us. We are meant to know that in all things he is working towards our supreme good.

My grandmother taught me as a child to say over my personal difficulties, 'It will pass.' This is not a passive resignation in the face of adverse circumstances. It is the rock solid faith that God is always working for our good. The events of Good Friday and Easter Day become the pattern not only for the Christian life but for the whole of the created order.

'Give God time,' I can hear her saying, 'he needs time to bring things to pass.' What else explains the interval of time between the Ascension of Christ and the glorious culmination of his work when the kingdom he has established comes in all its fullness.

Her phrase 'Give God time' lies at the heart of the story concerning Prime Minister Joseph in the book of Genesis. His jealous brothers had found a way of disposing of the priggish teenager in the family and he nearly lost his life in the events which followed. Missing, presumed dead, there was eventually a family reunion and the only way Joseph could interpret the amazing turn of fortune in his own life was to express: 'You intended to harm me but God, in his time, intended all that has happened for the blessing of many people.'

As I look back I realise that I received the greatest gift in my childhood. The Good News of Jesus Christ came to me in a context of warmth and wit, but above all the teaching of the Bible was conveyed in such a way that I knew it was pertinent to real life, and the people who surrounded me were free samples of what it meant to be a follower of Jesus Christ. It made sense. And although I did not realise it at the time, my grandmother's ongoing conversations with a child were an introduction to the jigsaw of life. She began the task of connecting the little pieces of a boy's life to that wider context which we have termed 'the map of meaning'.

My mother followed in the same tradition as my grandmother. She is a woman of great devotion to whom I owe so much in my life. She taught me a prayer whose words and melody, so I am told, were sung over my cradle from the day of my birth:

> Gentle Jesus, meek and mild,
> Look upon a little child,
> Pity my simplicity,
> Suffer me to come to thee.

And by God's grace, I did.

Creator God,
With your feet I walk,
I walk with your limbs,
I carry forth your body,
For me your mind thinks,
Your voice speaks for me.
Beauty is before me
And beauty is behind me,
Above and below me hovers the beautiful,
I am surrounded by it,
I am immersed in it.
In my youth I am aware of it,
And in my old age
I shall walk quietly
The beautiful trail.

Navaho blessing

When David Livingstone was ten years old he went to work in a factory as a piecer. The first half-crown he earned he gave to his mother. It was some years before he was promoted to be a spinner. He often looked back on those years of monotonous toil with gratitude. In them he learnt the secrets of faith and courage, which stood him in good stead in the wilds of Africa. Few men have been so honoured as he – explorer, doctor, missionary, faithful servant of God, and brother to all his fellow men. Yet once he stood as a lonely boy at a new job in a factory. Because he tackled the first job with faith and hope and courage, he did not fail in the last great adventure.

Leslie Church

The boys were isolated from their homes to a degree it is difficult to grasp. 'Left absolutely alone at eight years of age amidst the constant bustle of a great school,' wrote one who joined the school in 1843, 'I had a few days of utter misery. I have never known such a sense of utter desolation since. My home was utterly gone from me . . .' The journey had involved two days of travelling by coach; he was indeed the only boy who had so much as seen a railway train. There was no penny post; a letter home would cost a shilling; and even writing paper, sealing wax, and wafers were a costly luxury. To have sent a letter, whether home or elsewhere, without its being submitted to the censorship of the masters and the Governor would have been a crime certain to meet with condign punishment. No holidays long enough to give a chance of a visit home were to be expected until the midsummer vacation; and at that age nine months must have seemed an eternity.

A. G. Ives, *Kingswood School in Wesley's Day and Since*

There is something majestic about late Victorian Methodist piety even in its narrowness. A friend has told me how, as a boy, he was once staying in the home of his grandfather, a Methodist Minister, and a vivacious young aunt bought a pack of playing cards and was teaching him to play. When the grandfather discovered them at their game, he not only delivered a stern and sorrowful reproof, but retired to his study and spent two hours wrestling in prayer for their salvation.

Gordon Wakefield,
Methodist Devotion

Holy Child, of heavenly birth,
God made manifest on earth,
Fain I would thy follower be,
Live in everything like thee.

Thy humility impart;
Give me thy obedient heart,
Free and cheerful to fulfil
All my heavenly Father's will.

Keep me thus to God resigned,
Till his love delights to find
Fairly copied out on me
All the mind which was in thee.

Charles Wesley, A Child's Prayer

I would have given the church my head, my heart. She would not have them. She did not know what to do with them. She told me to go back and do crochet in my mother's drawing room; or if I were tired of that, to marry and look well at the head of my husband's table. You may go to the Sunday School if you like it, she said. But she gave me no training even for that. She gave me neither work to do for her, nor education for it.

Florence Nightingale

Clever people often scathingly criticise the youth of today for having 'no historic sense'. But surely that is hardly to be wondered at. So great and far-reaching have been the changes in modern life that the young person of today cannot see any but the slenderest connexion between what appears to him the slow, simple and secure life of a bygone generation and the highly complex, fast-moving life of the world today. The historic sense is often the fruit of maturity, and while an experienced Christian may be glad to think that he is worshipping the same God as did Abraham, Moses, David, and the saints of the Christian Church, the young person of today, even if he knows who Abraham, Moses and David were, will be quite unmoved by the historical connexion. His clamant need is for an adequate God of Today; the historic sense may well come later.

J. B. Phillips,
Your God is too Small

May the strength of God pilot us.
May the power of God preserve us.
May the wisdom of God instruct us.
May the hand of God protect us.
May the way of God direct us.
May the shield of God defend us.

from St Patrick's Breastplate

The average young person or adult spends at least half of his or her time in some form of work or serious activity.
It is only fitting that this should become the subject of our prayers.

Not in order to 'succeed' in the world's eyes, or to make more money, but to be fulfilled.
To be creative in our use of the talents and gifts God has given us.
To be thoughtful of others in the way we do our work.

. . . God *is* concerned about our work, as about the other aspects of our lives, and this should encourage us to bring our work into the divine presence when we pray.

Prayer relates our subconscious lives to our conscious lives. To brood about our work in prayer enables the Spirit to release hidden power and insight from the subconscious levels of our being, so that they may be used in doing our work.

. . . Thank God for your work, which is actually one of the greatest blessings of your life.

John Killinger, *Beginning Prayer*

I am Coming to You

Philip Jones

Like a traveller, boarding a train
For a surprise journey to long-lost friends,
I am coming to you.

Like money you never knew you had
That was stored deep in that coat pocket,
Or owed you by the taxman.
I am coming to you.

Like a burst of recognition
That lay hidden in your mind,
When suddenly memory turned the key
That made you say, 'Ah ... yes ... '
I am coming to you.

Like an unexpected shower out of a cloudless sky,
So that only Mother Nature
could have guessed the source,
I am coming to you.

I am coming to you as if God had winked
And in an instant
Altered creation ...

I am surprise.

You did not know – still less expect –
That, at the end of fruitlessness came the fertile crop,
That in the scorching desert heat of midday,
you'd find the oasis
Or that when hope and chance shrivelled together
Under the scorn of logic,
Would come certainty.

I am assurance.

I am God's laughter at the world.

I am Good News of Great Joy.

I am promise.

I am future.

I am your hope.

And my name is faith.

I stand on the doorstep of your lives
And the movements you feel within you
Are just the knocking of my tiny fist
On that door, saying

I AM COMING TO YOU.

You show me the path of life. In your presence there is fullness of joy; in your right hand are pleasures for evermore.

Psalm 16:11

SUMMER

Active, Hectic and Noisy!

Andrew Dyer

Religion has always been part of my life. Having a father who is a Methodist minister means that you can't really avoid it! Going to church on a Sunday was, to me, the most natural thing in the world. To most of my school friends this type of behaviour was strange, unusual and perhaps even unnatural. Growing up in a society where, as a Christian and a regular church-goer, you are in the minority, isn't easy. It may not be easy, but that doesn't mean that you should give up being 'different', just to fit in.

I remember getting a fair amount of stick at school about being a Christian. 'Bible-basher' was a common insult. At times I felt that it would have been interesting to see just what sort of damage a heavy copy of the Good News could do! Once people realise that their taunts aren't going to change what you believe, the novelty value tends to wear off and their attentions turn elsewhere.

My school days are well behind me now, and I am currently in my final year at the University of Brighton, studying for a degree in Accounting and Finance. Mention the word 'accountancy' and it's surprising the stereotypical responses you still get. The word 'boring' crops up more than any other. I'd like to take this opportunity to put the record straight. Accountancy is not boring, nor does it involve counting beans – just ask any accountant!

It's taken me four years to complete the course, rather than the standard three, because I decided to take up the sandwich option of the degree and spent the second half of 1994 and most of 1995 working for the Methodist Publishing House. I lived at home while I was working and this allowed me to become involved in the local MAYC group, Belvoir Link.

Another thing that is difficult to avoid, when your father is known as Rev. rather than Mr., is moving house. Thankfully ministerial moves are not as frequent as they traditionally were. We spent thirteen years in St Neots in Cambridgeshire before moving to the Vale of Belvoir Circuit, between Grantham and Nottingham, in 1993. We had only been in the area six weeks before I had to go back to university to start my second year, and so I hadn't had a chance to get involved in the MAYC group until I started at MPH.

I think 'lively' might be a good word to use to describe the group! Active, hectic and noisy are others that come easily to mind. As it is a rural area, the group has a circuit-wide membership. A minibus is used to transport members to and from meetings and as one of the more 'senior' members of the group I drive it fairly frequently. I haven't had any complaints about my driving – yet! This, along with helping to organise various events, is my way of giving something back to the group, which I feel is very important.

Throughout the year the group is involved in several events, but the highlight for most, including myself, is the annual MAYC London Weekend in May. For one weekend a year the residents of London are invaded by armies of green and yellow clad young people. The weekend often coincides with the FA Cup Final and it's amazing how often we get mistaken for football supporters! There tend to be a lot of puzzled faces trying to work out which team we support – especially when neither Cup finalist plays in green or yellow! We tell them that we are members of God's team, and that Jesus is our captain. That confuses them even more!

Belvoir Link have performed at the weekend twice, in the Saturday show in the Royal Albert Hall. I was lucky enough to be involved on the second of these occasions. The centrepiece of the performance was a thirty foot long Chinese dragon which entered the arena (helped by sixteen nervous Belvoir Link members concealed within) through the audience down a flight of steps. Quite an entrance! When you combine that with a live band of musicians playing oil drums and dustbin lids you begin to appreciate some of the slightly unusual things we get up to!

There is no doubt in my mind that the weekend is special. There is no other atmosphere that compares to it. Despite the emphasis on having fun, the central purpose is clear: to worship God. I have felt closer to God during these weekends than at any other times during my life. A piece in last year's worship service combined the crucifixion scene from *Jesus of Nazareth* with the Bryan Adams song '(Everything I Do) I Do It For You'. If you've got the song, (and most of you must have it, judging by the length of time it was number one!) listen to the words next time you play it and relate them to the life of Jesus. The experience still gives me goose bumps when I think about it and really brought home the ultimate sacrifice one man had made for me.

Many people worry about the future of the Church. There is no denying that there is cause for concern. The biggest problem, in my mind, is the style and content of worship. Young people are just not attracted to worship because they do not find it interesting, relevant or stimulating.

The outlook is not so black, and you need look no further than the London Weekend to know that the Methodist Church contains vibrant, passionate and energetic young people. The challenge is to ensure that these young people continue to develop their Christian lives when they leave their teenage years and MAYC behind.

Now I'm back in Brighton things are quite different. With two universities and a College of Technology there ought to be plenty of young Christians in Brighton. Well, if there are they're doing a very good job of hiding! For many, university brings with it a first taste of real freedom. With that freedom comes a whole new range of opportunities and possibilities. All too often religion is not on the agenda anymore and other things take priority. I have tried the University's Christian Union, and didn't really fit in. I have attended the local Methodist Church, but this year there are just no young people at all. The contrast couldn't, therefore, be greater. I have been used to being surrounded by my friends each week, and now there is no one of my age.

The final year of my degree has been a combination of working hard on my studies, and working equally hard trying to find a job. The economy is such that I'm not in a position to be too choosy about where I end up working, be it North, South, East or West – any job is a blessing. This makes my immediate future very uncertain. Facing that future knowing that I have God's help and guidance is a great comfort. People have asked me whether that future might include following in my father's footsteps and joining the ministry. It's OK living with a minister, but being one . . . that's a whole new ball game! (Sorry, Dad.)

Wherever I end up and whatever I end up doing, the Church will always be part of my life. I realise that I have much to learn about my beliefs and the Christian faith, and for me the only way to learn is to be involved (even if it's not from the pulpit!). I would like to continue working with young people. After all, the young people of today will be the backbone of the Church tomorrow. If my experiences of today's young Methodists are anything to go by then the future's bright, the future's dynamic and above all the future has God placed firmly at the centre of life. But isn't that the way it should be anyway?

Every year after the long strain of winter our whole being begins to ache for all that the summer means. Quiet Sunday afternoons, for instance, with a book on a secluded lawn, the shadow of beeches on the grass, and the clouds floating slowly across the blue above our heads, the silence defined rather than broken by the occasional hum of a bee passing from flower to flower. 'Like a walled-in garden to a troubled mind.' What a description of the peace of God! I know some gardens that seem to have about them a secret peace in which the whole personality seems bathed and restored.

Leslie D. Weatherhead,
Jesus and Ourselves

O God, of whose gift come sunshine, and friendship, and the glory of a summer's day, who in the common things of daily life givest to us thy very Self, making of bread and wine the sacrament of thy sustaining presence; strengthen and refresh us that we may seek thee eagerly, find thee surely, and serve thee faithfully, through Jesus Christ our Lord.

Source unknown

Woman was made from the rib of man.
She was not created from his head – to top him,
nor from his feet – to be stepped upon.

She was made from his side – to be equal to him;
from beneath his arm – to be protected by him:
near his heart – to be loved by him.

                                        Anonymous

Where does the family start? It starts with a young man falling in love with a girl – no superior alternative has yet been found.

                                        Winston Churchill

When the late Mr and Mrs Henry Ford celebrated their golden wedding anniversary, a reporter asked them, 'To what do you attribute your fifty years of successful life?'

'The formula,' said Ford, 'is the same formula I have always used in making cars – just stick to one model.'

                                        Anonymous

Married couples who love each other tell each other a thousand things without talking.

Chinese proverb

There are certain personal attitudes and feelings that contribute to creative relationships with others. They include, for one thing, warm acceptance and understanding instead of rejection or hostility. Even when we disagree with or regret the action of another, we can emphasise 'I still love you,' instead of 'You really were a fool.' When disagreement is called for, we can be honest and open instead of masked and hidden. Instead of remaining silent, we can speak out when a different position needs to be expressed. But such a reaction can be held within a framework of basic support for the other. We can help others feel that we are still on their side when it comes to appreciating and encouraging them as persons.

Harvey and Lois Seifert,
Liberation of Life

Love is an act of endless forgiveness, a tender look which becomes a habit.

Peter Ustinov

A cloudless sky, a world of heather,
Purple of foxglove, yellow of broom;
We two among it, wading together;
Shaking out honey, treading perfume.
Crowds of bees are giddy with clover,
Crowds of grasshoppers skip at our feet,
Crowds of larks at their matins hang over,
Thanking the Lord for a life so sweet.

Jean Ingelow

At the time of his marriage, Thomas Jackson was receiving the then unusual wage of three pounds a week, and promotion awaited him. Suddenly, a call came to him to serve as circuit missionary. With a facetiousness which he still adopts in broaching important projects, he put the matter to his wife: 'Well, my dear, what about keeping house on a pound a week instead of three pounds?'

The answer was serious enough: 'If I have you, Tom, and it is the will of Jesus, I shall be as content to keep house with one as with three pounds a week.'

William Potter,
Thomas Jackson of Whitechapel

The Lord sanctify and bless you,
The Lord pour the riches of his grace upon you
that you may please him
and live together in holy love
to your lives' end.
So be it.

John Knox, blessing for a wedding

Once an older man came to talk with me about the pain he had experienced for several years when he discovered his wife had been unfaithful to him. He was a long-standing church member and sincere believer in prayer and the love of God. He couldn't understand why he couldn't really forgive his wife and let the past go.

'I love her,' he told me, with tears in his eyes. 'I never wanted a divorce. She's a wonderful woman in so many ways, and I know I was partly to blame. But I can't let it go. I can't stop thinking about it. I'm still resentful, even though I want to forgive. I've prayed and prayed about it, and it doesn't seem to make any difference. But we're told by Jesus that we must forgive. Well, I've tried, but it just doesn't happen.'

As we shared and talked together, it became clear to us both after a while that by his wish to forgive, his willingness, he had in fact forgiven her. But the feeling of forgiveness and release would probably not come until his pain had been healed.

Flora Slosson Wuellner, *Prayer, Stress*
and our Inner Wounds

The Christian in Politics

Bernard Weatherill

If what Christians say about God is true, then everything in life matters to him. On that basis alone it can be maintained that politics matter to God and that they should therefore matter to the people of God. As Max Warren has put it:

> God is a God of politics. For to worship in Church a God who is not a God of politics and who is not as much concerned with what happens in the market-place as what takes place in the sanctuary, is to worship an idol and not a living God.

Christians must therefore get involved or else abandon all political influence to agnostics and atheists. To be in public life is to have an opportunity to influence people and events on a great scale. In our lifetime the State has become the most comprehensive institution of society. This being so, the Christian cannot justifiably ignore politics any more than he can avoid politics as a citizen. In many parts of the world the State has become the most threatening incarnation of the Prince of Darkness. Great segments of mankind live constantly on the brink of disaster because political power is in the hands of godless politicians. Christians therefore have a duty to involve themselves in politics;

to ensure that political power is wielded with wisdom and compassion, and, above all, to ensure that it is used to liberate and not to enslave. The modern politician has the power to influence so many of the evils that have cursed mankind for countless generations. No Christian is entitled to curse darkness when it is possible for him to carry such a torch!

In Lamb's biography of Alexander the Great, he recalls that in the course of one campaign Alexander and his generals sat down to study their charts and found to their astonishment that they had marched completely off the map! To a large degree this is true of the age in which we are now privileged to live. Our modern 'torches' shed precious little light on the enormous changes – political, economic and technological – we are likely to see in the rest of our lifetime.

But Christians do have a chart and one which has never failed them – the Bible and the Ten Commandments. All of us in life, and especially in public life, have a duty to set an example in our private lives, and, what is more, the electorate has a right to expect it from us. In my visits to schools I always remind young people of 'the five Rs' – Reading, Writing, Arithmetic and Right and Wrong!

The cornerstone of good government has always been good people – not just at the top but in all levels of society.

To make a Nation truly great, a handful of heroes capable of great deeds at supreme moments is not enough. Heroes are not always available, and one can often do without them. But it is essential to have millions of reliable people. Honest citizens who steadfastly place the public interest before their own.

Pasquale Vilari, 1826-1918.

King Solomon, faced with similar problems to our own, prayed not for power to overcome them, but for the wisdom to know the difference between right and wrong. Nothing that is morally wrong can ever be politically right. If Christians subject every political decision to that test, we shall have a country which, in the beautiful words of the Communion Service, is 'godly and quietly governed'.

Yes, I remember Adlestrop
The name, because one afternoon
Of heat, the express train drew up there
Unwontedly. It was late June.

The steam hissed. Someone cleared his throat.
No-one left and no-one came
On the bare platform. What I saw
Was Adlestrop — only the name

And willows. Willow herb and grass,
And meadowsweet, and haycocks dry
No whit less still and lonely fair
Than the high cloudlets in the sky.

And for that minute a blackbird sang
Close by, and round him, mistier,
Farther and farther, all the birds
Of Oxfordshire and Gloucestershire.

Edward Thomas

Marriage is an empty box. It remains empty unless you put in more than you take out.

Anonymous

It was in the desert that the Hebrews were found by God. Whereas in Eygpt and Sumeria nature had a soothing rhythm and offered abundant crops, and man was absorbed into the divine system and surrounded by it, the wilderness offered no such sense of security. In that stark solitude God was not a part of the world around: he was above it and very different from it. The Hebrew did not contemplate God – he heard his voice and his command in the thunder of the hills and in the fearsome voices of the night. The wilderness bred not the carefully organised life of the agricultural community, but a strong individualism, a life of constant action and decision, which involved the man who was alone upon the hills where danger and death lurked. These men found that God was not a theory or a general scheme which enveloped the whole of life for the whole cycle of days, but a strongly individual God who dealt with separate men and women – with Jacob, with Moses, with Samuel and Elijah and Hosea.

John Baker

There are two sorts of constancy in love; the one comes from the constant discovery in our beloved of new grounds for love, and the other comes from making it a point of honour to be constant.

Francois Rouchefoucauld

Jesus too was perfectly at home in the world of the emotions. His relationship with women was without a practising sexuality because what he had to do could only be done alone, just as some people are still called to a single state in order to fulfil a particular task (or others suffer it because they have lost the one they loved). Yet he was free enough with women to cause grave scandal and he had special friends among them, like Mary Magdalen who in the garden of the resurrection was specifically asked by Jesus not to touch him for the obvious reason that she went to give him a hug as she had always done.

Hugh Buckingham, *Feeling Good*

When we recently stayed for a few days with our son he showed us a ship that he was in the process of making for his three-year-old child. What had started as a roughly-fashioned piece of wood, something to play with in the bath, manufactured in an odd moment from an offcut left over after some serious, necessary, tedious, household repair, was becoming a beautiful little ship, hollowed out as a ferry for toy cars, with hinged doors, and a real captain's bridge, and wheel, and capstan and anchor and a deck with rails. By becoming as a little child and entering into its kingdom, however momentarily, this father had been inspired to work long and carefully on a toy which was as good as he could make it, a toy which could be used in all sorts of imaginative play; a toy created with love.

Nancy Blamires, Looking on Glass

For the beauty of the earth,
    For the beauty of the skies,
For the love which from our birth
    Over and around us lies:

Gracious God, to thee we raise
This our sacrifice of praise.

For the beauty of each hour
    Of the day and of the night,
Hill and vale, and tree and flower,
    Sun and moon and stars of light:

For the joy of ear and eye,
    For the heart and mind's delight,
For the mystic harmony
    Linking sense to sound and sight:

For the joy of human love,
    Brother, sister, parent, child,
Friends on earth and friends above,
    For all gentle thoughts and mild:

For each perfect gift of thine
    To our race so freely given,
Graces human and divine,
    Flowers of earth and buds of heaven:

Folliott Sandford Pierpoint

Within minutes of [Eva Burrows'] birth into a Salvation Army family, her officer father had dedicated his newborn baby girl to the glory of God and the salvation of the world. Perhaps it was to be expected then that she would receive a 'divine compulsion' to enter the Army at the age of nineteen, despite having gone through the usual teenage rejections of her religious heritage. For Eva Burrows, this calling was as real and as intimate as it is possible to experience. In her own words, 'I dedicated my mind as well as every part of my temperament and personality, which included the giving up of marriage.'

Thus it was with total dedication that Eva Burrows entered on her career in the Army, devoting all her time and energy to her work and the people under her care. The Army is her family. It is the 'vibrant warmth' of the affection between them which is the mainstay of her strength. She can truly say, 'God is no-one's debtor; what I may have given up for him, he has given back a hundred times over.'

Interview with Eva Burrows
(formerly General of the Salvation Army)

Action may not always bring happiness;
but there is no happiness without action.

Benjamin Disraeli

Mid-life, the Itinerant Ministry and Teenage Daughters

Stephen Dawes

This is the story of one ministerial family between 1989 and 1995, a time which for us was occasionally dramatic, frequently traumatic, and mostly that blend of the ordinarily problematic which constitutes normality.

I see myself as a traditional circuit minister even though I have served as often outside circuits (theological colleges in Ghana 1980 and Birmingham 1988, and the Cornwall District chairmanship 1992) as in them (Hexham 1971, Stafford 1976, Bodmin 1984). Margaret and I were married when I left college and Margaret chose to devote herself entirely to the raising of a family if it arrived and to voluntary work in the church and outside it. Carolyn was born in 1973 and Alison in 1976.

The story begins in 1989, but looking back we can see two hints of what was to come. In 1976 we moved to Stafford and Ali became one of those babies who did not sleep at night, resulting in eighteen wearying months for the rest of us. Our four years in Ghana were remarkably happy and fulfilling despite the extreme difficulties of living there during the country's economic collapse, and Ali found the return to England very difficult. It took her two years to settle, maybe because Ghana was the only home she really remembered or because her life there was one of such fun, freedom and friendships. But settle she did. Then six months later I received a 'phone call saying that I was to be nominated as the Old Testament tutor at Queen's College in Birmingham.

Margaret and I share the same view of ministry and ordination; that ordination means putting oneself at the disposal of the Church, and that ministry means serving Christ in the Church and the world first with questions of personal fulfilment and satisfaction second. This is an old-fashioned view, but for us it is central to our discipleship as Christians, and it is summed up in the words of the Methodist Covenant Service, 'Put me to what you will, rank me with whom you will.' So in 1988 we went to Queen's.

By any account theological colleges are odd places, but despite the peculiarities and frustrations of Queen's I had four rewarding years there. Carolyn enjoyed Birmingham too. Not so Margaret or Ali. Margaret had taken the opportunities presented by being a superintendent minister's wife in Cornwall to play a full part in the life of the local church and circuit, and in addition had been very busy promoting Traidcraft across the county. At Queen's a tutor's wife was expected to be neither seen nor heard. She did something to change that and also became involved in Traidcraft in Birmingham, but the four years were not good, compounded by health problems which led to a hysterectomy. It was Ali, however, who found it all too much. We still do not know quite how or why, but the thing that seemed to throw her already uncertain life into turmoil was the break-up of a marriage on the campus. There had been increasing difficulty in getting her to go to school and in December 1989 she stopped altogether. She didn't return until the following September. At home she was withdrawn though never hostile. She was obviously deeply sad, but couldn't share it, and we couldn't get through it. She would go out with us to see family or old friends, and would see her own friends on the campus and go to the College youth fellowship: but nothing more, except to go to the local chapel youth group. She remained the strongly self-willed person she had always been, but at the same time she was utterly lacking in self-confidence; that sounds an odd combination, but it is the only way I can describe it.

The tale of the next ten months can be briefly told but it felt like an age at the time. She wasn't any problem at home, except that she was there! In the spring we attended family counselling, the counsellor in front with a team behind the screen and all that, which was a complete waste of time. The counsellor never talked to Ali at all, only to Margaret and me, it being clearly perceived that whatever was wrong was our fault. Salvation came in two ways; firstly in the home tutor who came after Easter, a Methodist from a local church! She was superb. When Ali did go back to school to begin her GCSE course this teacher met her every lunchtime for the first fortnight, and then one evening a week for the next two years, ostensibly to help her with maths. Secondly, help was provided indirectly by the Chairman of the District who reminded me about the psychiatrist the District used from time to time. We took Ali to this person, without charge, on and off for two years. This support, encouragement and friendship enabled Ali to return to school and to cope when she did.

Just after Ali returned to school, I received the news that I had been nominated and then shortlisted for the Chairmanship of the Cornwall District, a job I had not sought and didn't fancy. Move or stay? The question of what this change would do to Ali was a big one, but there was also a dilemma involving Carolyn, who would be, at that point, in the middle of a BTec course. We decided that despite all of this there was no way that we could or would say no to the Church if the Church decided that this was the job for us, which it did.

The move to Cornwall was the next stage of Ali's salvation, for from the first day in Truro she felt she had come 'home'. It was not so for Carolyn. We left her at Queen's. She had been looking forward to independence but the combination of the lonely life of a bedsit plus the fact that her boyfriend had gone to university at Southampton meant an unhappy year. The break-up of that relationship led to a phone call that she had taken an overdose and was in hospital. After that she moved into a friend's home for the rest of the term, then came to us in Truro.

Carolyn had always wanted to be a nurse, and in the year she had to wait before she could apply she looked for a job as a care assistant. She had several, losing each one when back problems from an old accident manifested themselves. This too made nursing impossible. She was unemployed, but then she met

Brian, a local unemployed graduate. A couple of months later they announced that they were going to Plymouth to look for jobs and to live together. I saw nothing wrong in the arrangement; Margaret found it less easy to accept, but neither of us opposed it and on moving day we put our not inconsiderable moving experience to good use. We could not have opposed their decision, for we had always tried to enable the girls to make their own decisions and stand by them.

We had not, for example, insisted on their attending church and had not pressed the Christian faith upon them. The result was that Carolyn had become a member of the Methodist Church and Ali, whilst having declined to be a member, was a regular attender at worship and at most things to do with the church's youth work in Truro. So Carolyn and Brian moved to Plymouth and began life together in a dreadful Rachmanesque flat. Some of Brian's family found this difficult, not least in understanding how a Methodist minister could not only accept that his daughter was living with her boyfriend but even be positive about it.

How so? One of the courses I shared in at Queen's involved looking at marriage and the Bible. The Bible contains no definition of marriage, and the only one you can distil from it is that marriage is 'socially-recognised pair-bonding'. Our traditional English Church definition of marriage as 'one man and one woman for life', following a church service, is our own cultural tradition, and other Christians in other places do things differently. In Ghana, for example, I saw that you get married in three ways: 'by local law and custom', 'under the ordinance' and 'in church', and these three may be years apart! So, as I saw it from the Bible's point of view, when Carolyn and Brian went to live together they were not 'living in sin' or cohabiting – these are our terms not the Bible's – but actually beginning their married life! Here was a test. Would this theology survive outside the classroom, especially when it involved my own daughter? It did.

To bring that story up to date. They were obviously right for each other and decided to get married, and it was my privilege to conduct their wedding in March 1995. That summer they moved to a rented house and Brian's temporary job eventually became as permanent as anything can be these days. Carolyn is now happily doing a degree course at Plymouth. There were times when so much attention was given to her sister, or when she was asserting her independence that we didn't know who she was and the relationship became distant, even difficult. No doubt that process is an inevitable part of parenting and adolescence: but now we can rejoice in a good and open relationship.

Back to Ali. She now commutes daily to the same university. It had to be Plymouth because she could not face moving out of Cornwall. Ali needs roots, that much has become clear, and she has already begun to worry about what will happen when we leave Truro. We hope that our purchase of a little terraced house in Truro for our retirement – the tenant pays the mortgage! – will give her some of the security she needs. There are still times when we do not know who Ali really is, and when we feel excluded from her life and she from ours, but no doubt that too is part of the ongoing pain of parenthood and of her own ongoing search for herself.

So where was God in all this? There were times when we asked that question, and when we raged at his absence. Religious platitudes never helped. What did was belonging to a network of caring people. Above all, it helped to remember who we were, disciples and followers of Jesus. The title of Bonhoeffer's book, *The Cost of Discipleship*, came frequently to mind, as did the words of the Covenant Service. So despite the cost, and our feelings of guilt that some of the cost of our discipleship has actually been paid by our children, we would not have it any other way. As I have written elsewhere:

> Those words (of the Covenant Service) still express for me the discipline of obedience and discipleship to which Christ has called me and all of us, and I hope and pray that by his generous love and care Margaret and I will continue to be able to live by them, in the spirit of the old Handsworth motto, 'Where the Lord leads'.

Lord, grant that I may always desire more than I can accomplish.

Michelangelo

The only time that is fully real is the present. Yesterday is old news and tomorrow is full of maybes. This is obvious enough, when one reflects on it, but it takes many years to realise its full implications. So most of us spend a great deal of our time daydreaming about the past or worrying about the future. Not realising the value of the real bird we have in hand, we leave the present to go rooting in past or future bushes. As a result the personal business that should stand highest on our agenda often never gets done. What is this personal business? Finding peace of mind, and so happiness, here and now. Learning to live so that we savour each day, wasting none of the precious moments God has given us.

John Carmody, *How to Make It Through the Day*

It is not enough to have a good mind; the main thing is to use it well.

Descartes

O you gotta get a Glory in the work you do,
An Hallelujah Chorus in the heart of you.
Paint, or tell a story, sing, or shovel coal,
O you gotta get a Glory, or the job lacks soul.
O Lord, give me a Glory — is it too much to give?
For you gotta get a Glory, or you just don't live.

The great, whose shining labours make our
    pulses throb,
Were men who got a Glory in their daily job.
The battle might be gory, and the odds unfair,
But the men who got a Glory never knew despair.
O Lord, give me a Glory — when all else is done,
If you've only got a Glory, you can still go on.

For those who get a Glory, it is like the sun,
And you can see it glowing through the work
    they've done.
O fame is transitory — riches fade away —
But when you've got a Glory, it is there to stay.
O Lord, give me a Glory, and a workman's pride,
For you gotta get a Glory, or you're dead inside.

                    Lines written by the black commander of
                        a paddle steamer on the Great Lakes

Will you notice, in the first place, that Jesus' hands were *toil-worn* hands. The soldier noticed it; the soldier who nailed him to the wood. As he stretched his arm along the cross-beam, and pointed his nail at the palm, it struck him – this was not the hand of some sedentary worker; this was not the hand of some habitué of the Court. This was the toil-worn hand of a working man.

Notice that. Jesus was a working man. Oh! you don't realise the wonder of that until you think yourself back into the Greek and Roman world and consider their attitude to manual work. They despised it. It was the occupation of slaves. Plato and Aristotle were both great and clever men, but to both of them manual work was a thing of near-contempt. It was not an occupation for free men; it was a task only for the slave.

And this was God's answer to that; his reply to the ancient world's contempt for manual work. Peep into the carpenter's shop at Nazareth and see the incarnate Son of God bending his back at a bench; see him ankle-deep in the shavings and perspiring as he toils. This is the answer of Almighty God to those who despise manual work.

W. E. Sangster,
Westminster Sermons (vol i)

Pride makes us do things well. But it is love that makes us do them to perfection.

Anonymous

Happy the man, whose wish and care
  A few paternal acres bound,
Content to breathe his native air
  In his own ground.

Whose herds with milk, whose fields with bread,
  Whose flocks supply him with attire,
Whose trees in summer yield him shade,
  In winter fire.

Blest, who can unconcernd'ly find
  Hours, days, and years, slide soft away,
In health of body, peace of mind,
  Quiet by day,

Sound sleep by night; study and ease
  Together mix'd; sweet recreation,
And innocence, which most does please
  With meditation.

Thus let me live, unseen, unknown;
  Thus unlamented let me die;
Steal from the world, and not a stone
  Tell where I lie.

                              Alexander Pope

from Disguises of Love

Eddie Askew

When people learn that my major leisure activity is painting pictures, a common response is: 'It must be very relaxing.' Which shows how little many folk know about painting! It may be relaxing if your aims are not too high, but if you seriously want to accomplish something then it's hard work. I occasionally spend a week painting with a professional painter. We spend eight to ten hours a day out in the open – wind, rain and sun, standing with our easels, analysing form and colour in landscape and trying to get it down in paint. 'There is nothing between you and success,' said John Rogers, the painter, 'except what happens between your brush and the canvas.' True, but brush and paint seem to have a life of their own and don't always conform to the painter's dream.

Last time, we had two other people with us – an elderly married couple who had a rather romantic dream of painting. They came thinking that they could learn a few rules of perspective, colour mixing and so on – a few tricks of the trade – which would enable them to turn out competent paintings at will. It was painful for them as their illusions were slowly stripped away and they came face to face with reality. The reality is that painting is a discipline which demands regular application, hard work and practice over the years if you are going to be able to communicate something worthwhile. I think they may have learned more about themselves than about painting in the week we were together.

The Christian life is the same, there is no easy way. Rules there are, as a foundation to build on, but you don't develop and grow just by following a set of rules. Discipline and hard work come in. Paul's reference to athletics is relevant: '. . . all the runners run the race, though only one wins the prize . . . But every athlete goes into strict training . . .' (I Cor. 9: 24, 25 NEB). 'Run with resolution . . .' says Hebrews 12:1.

Training and resolution are the requirements for anything worth doing – painting, language, learning, athletics, Christian living. There are no short cuts. But that's not all. The greatest technician in painting is cold without a spark of sensitivity, perception, genius, which breathes life into what he creates. It's something which can't be measured or explained, but it can be recognised and accepted gladly when it's there. That's the Spirit. Whether inspiring the painter's vision or filling the Christian's life with joy, it is the Spirit who turns the pedestrian into the inspiring, who transforms the rules – the dead letter of the law – into life-giving freedom. God grant it to each one of us, together with the discipline to persevere.

Lord, they're not easy,
the demands you make.
You come into my life
bringing joy and freedom and peace.
And it feels good.
But that's only the beginning.
Because along with that
you ask for commitment.
For loyalty. Discipline.
For all my time and energy.
My abilities, to be used in your work.
I'm no longer my own, but yours.

I never know what will happen next
on the road you've shaped for me.
I only know you make demands.
For some it's martyrdom. Suffering.
For some it's publicity. Or politics.
Maybe that's a kind of martyrdom
for those who do it honestly.
For most of us
it's just the struggle to keep our balance
as we walk along the footpath of faith.

I can't see very far ahead.
Maybe that's just as well.
If I knew what was coming,
good or not so good,
I'd only worry,
and try to change it.
Help me, Lord,
to put one step in front of the other
as I follow your lead.
I know you can.
Because wherever I go, you've already been.
Wherever I go, you are already there.
And with me on the journey.
It's good to know that, to experience it.

And Lord, help me to find the joy
that comes with answering your demands.
Help me to live the freedom
that comes from walking in your love.
Help me to know the peace of your spirit.

E. A.

'What do *you* do for a living?' asked the friendly snack-bar waitress who had just served me with coffee.

'I'm a newspaper reporter on the editorial staff of the *Methodist Recorder* – a paper dealing with church matters in general and the Methodist Church in particular,' I replied.

She carefully considered this information for a few seconds. Then she said,

'What a funny sort of job.'

> Douglas J. Cock,
> *Every Other Inch a Methodist*

The old story of the man who, when he was asked what work he did for God, replied, 'I bake bread', and who would not be shifted from his answer by being told that he was expected to name some more 'spiritual' occupation, emphasises an essential point. God is concerned about his children's daily bread, and how shall he answer their prayers for it if there are none who will enter his service as farmers, millers, bakers, transport-workers, shopkeepers?

> Alan Kay

Father God,
Why is it that I think I must get somewhere, assume
    some position, be gathered together, or separated
    apart in the quiet of my study to pray?

Why is it that I feel I have to go somewhere or do some
    particular act to find you, reach you, and talk with
    you?

Your presence is here
    In the city – on the busy bus, in the factory, in the
    cockpit of the airplane, in the hospital – in the
    patients' rooms, in the intensive care unit, in the
    waiting room; in the home – at dinner, in the
    bedroom, in the family room, at my workbench; in
    the car – in the car park, at the traffic light.

Lord, reveal your presence to me everywhere, and help
    me become aware of your presence each moment
    of the day.

May your presence fill the nonanswers, empty glances,
    and lonely times of my life.

Robert Wood,
A Thirty-Day Experiment in Prayer

*Once while St Francis of Assisi was hoeing his garden, he was asked,
'What would you do if you were suddenly to learn that you were to
die at sunset today?' He replied, 'I would finish hoeing my garden.'*

Anonymous

Yellow with birdfoot-trefoil are the grass glades;
Yellow with cinquefoil of the dew-grey leaf;
Yellow with stonecrop, the moss mounds are yellow;
Blue-necked the wheat sways, yellowing to the sheaf.
Green-yellow, bursts from the copse the laughing yaffle,
Sharp as a sickle is the edge of shade and shine.
Earth in her heart laughs, looking at the heavens,
Thinking of the harvest, I look and think of mine.

George Meredith

We rode through the pleasant and fruitful Carse of Gowry, a plain fifteen or sixteen miles long, between the river Tay and the mountains, very thick inhabited, to Perth. In the afternoon we walked over to the royal palace at Scone. It is a large old house, delightfully situated, but swiftly running to ruin. Yet there are a few good pictures, and some fine tapestry left, in what they call the Queen's and the King's chambers. And what is far more curious, there is a bed and a set of hangings in the (once) royal apartment, which was wrought by poor Queen Mary, while she was imprisoned in the castle of Lochleven. It is some of the finest needlework I ever saw, and plainly shows both her exquisite skill and unwearied industry.

John Wesley

Dear God, be good to me. The sea is so wide, and my boat is so small.

Breton Fisherman's prayer.

The diary also mentions other private activities not often evident in the more public accounts of Wesley's life as a young man. He constructs an arbour at Epworth, helps the workmen build his house in Savannah, works in his garden in Georgia, and plants trees at Wroot. He goes fishing with Thomas Hawkins and pares apples with Benjamin Ingham. As a student at Oxford, he exercises with frequent walks around Christ Church meadow and occasional games of tennis . . .

. . . Some of the activities listed in his diary are similar in nature to some noted in his *Journal*. But without the diary we would not have known that Wesley saw a performance of *Hamlet* at Goodman's Fields Playhouse in London or that he heard Handel direct a performance of the oratorio *Esther* at the theatre in Oxford.

Richard P. Heitzenrater,
'Wesley and his Diary',
John Wesley: Contemporary Perspectives

Let the blessing of St Peter's Master be . . . upon all that are lovers of virtue; and dare trust in his providence; and be quiet; and go a - angling.

Izaak Walton, The Compleat Angler

I asked God for strength that I might achieve;
I was made weak that I might learn humbly to obey.

I asked for help that I might do greater things;
I was given infirmity that I might do better things.

I asked for riches that I might be happy;
I was given poverty that I might be wise.

I asked for power that I might have the praise of others;
I was given weakness that I might feel the need of God.

I asked for all things that I might enjoy life;
I was given life that I might enjoy all things.

I got nothing that I asked for – but everything I'd hoped for.
My unspoken prayers were answered.
I am among all men most richly blessed!

An unknown soldier,
19th century

Gates

Les Wallace

I said to the man who stood at the gate of the
year, 'Give me a light that I may tread safely
into the unknown.' And he replied, 'Go out
into the darkness and put your hand into the
hand of God. That shall be to you better than a
light and safer than a known way.'

Minnie Louise Haskin

It was never pointed out to me when I became a
member of the Methodist Church in 1970 that the word
'gate' would come to mean so much to me in my
spiritual journey. I had come to the local church via
the MAYC youth club, and the church seemed to be an
extension of the club with more emphasis on worship
and not so much on table tennis, snooker, Curly
Wurlys and Coke (the drink!). Beliefs, doctrine and
creeds, as well as the unique aspects of Methodism,
had been discussed at membership preparation classes
and it all sounded OK. On the big day I received the
revered *Book of Offices* – the forerunner of the *Methodist
Service Book*. There followed a time of enjoyable
involvement with the church although God did not
seem to feature a great deal.

Along came marriage and relocation to another part of
the country. At this stage in my life I realised for the
first time that we can be drawn, called, badgered,

coerced, pressed, whatever one likes to call it, into God's service. Perhaps some of those descriptions sound a bit ridiculous; however, if one has made the decision to follow Christ, to become one of his disciples, one also has to accept the discipline that goes with that decision. Some may argue that to rise to a challenge may be simply to placate one's conscience, or to seek approval from others. Or is God showing us a gate through which we should pass if we are willing to do his will?

At this time my wife Dianne and I lived in the city centre of Norwich. We had been told, via the ol' grape vine, that people were required to lead the Sunday school and start a youth club in a growing outlying village north of the city. We both felt that this was something we could be involved with; we had taken part in several relevant courses and felt that if it was right for us to offer then we would be accepted.

As we were the only people to offer we were accepted! It felt right. The chapel society, though it was small, was receptive to new approaches which we hoped and prayed would enable all ages to feel welcome. There followed for us a time of discovery, and a growing spiritual awareness. There also followed: a baby, moving house, another baby and moving house again. I am relieved to say that pattern did not continue!

Then, when we were in south Norfolk, gates seemed to be high on the agenda, mainly from a practical point of view. We were living in our dream clay lump cottage with a small inglenook fireplace complete with 'Bessemer Beam', a frozen toilet in hard winters and room for a goat. The gates were to restrain the various livestock that we had chosen to share our lives with. The problem was that with my full time employment, family and animal husbandry, actually moving along on the road of discipleship seemed to have ceased. My life had become unbalanced. I was still involved in the church and doing youth work, but I felt that I had stopped growing. I needed time to think, time to get back in touch with God, time to listen to what he may have to say to me.

This stage came at a time when I was planning a business venture which was proceeding well. I started to set aside some time to think and to pray. My prayers were of a brief spur-of-the-moment nature with a little time for listening built in. It was hard at first because this exercise did not come naturally. I was out of touch with God, and spiritually unfit. After several months of inconsistent seeking there came a time when I was struck by the thought that it would be totally wrong for me to pursue the business venture.

It is difficult to describe how this thought came about. I tried to analyse why; perhaps I was getting cold feet? But something, someone – God? – was saying to me that this is not the way I want you to go and I could see that particular gate of opportunity closing before my mind's eye. And I backed away from all the planned activity of new business and instead tried to find God's way.

When this situation was put before my then superintendent minister he suggested some avenues to explore including full-time ministry of some sort, but also threw in, 'Have you considered training to become a local preacher?' This question hit me like a bolt out of the blue, it was so unexpected. I don't mind being challenged, but let's be serious! A great deal of thought followed; the prospect of studying and exams seemed very high hurdles to jump over for a non-academic animal such as I am.

I thought, I prayed and I listened, and I applied to start training, supervised by a great encourager who knew the art of emphasising the positive points of my early attempts and playing down the negative. The biggest miracle for me was that I found I could study, retain information and, to cap it all, pass exams, which I had never thought possible, feelings justified by my abysmal school career. I had passed through another gate into the next stage of my life: training going reasonably well, leading worship without supervision, now perhaps for a settled period.

Another chat with my superintendent. (Thought afterwards – must stop these little chats, they're disruptive!) Had I thought any more about the full time ministry? Possibly the Methodist Diaconal Order. 'But they wear dresses, don't they?' I said naively, and was told that I wouldn't have to wear a dress because men were now able to candidate for the Order. I admit that I was on the look-out for gates on the horizon but thought along the lines that the ones that had been suggested were most likely out of reach.

Off I went again to think, pray and listen. A point was reached when it seemed right to pursue that way ahead; however I found myself in a state of behind-the-scenes panic. It was like a nightmare, as though I was running round a field in despair looking for any gate to escape through but that one. Dianne and I found ourselves at a Ministries Day in Cambridge. I knew then that I had to candidate for the Order. Nothing else seemed right.

God was asking me to step through a gate into the unknown and to ask my family to come with me.

It's strange to think that one of the most exciting days of my life was when I received a letter in April 1991 accepting me for training for something which I was not sure I could carry out, certainly not in my own strength.

From candidating to being placed in my first appointment I have had to pray the hardest and listen more carefully than at any other time of my life for God's guidance, for there have come in that period of three years the most searching questions about myself, my faith and, at times, my doubts. As a family we have learnt much about tolerance and about supporting each other when one starts to fall by the wayside.

As Christians we cannot check the path at every footfall after passing through the gate to see if we can cope, but we can step forward boldly in faith, knowing that God will equip us for anything he asks us to do, and knowing that we walk the winding path of discipleship hand-in-hand with our loving Father.

A Meditation

Here I find myself standing at the gate of the future.
When I look down I see the stone slabs,
that are solid and sure beneath my feet.
Around the solid edges, though, there are weeds
and vines that will in time grow up
and wind round my body;
climbing, entwining, choking and hindering,
maybe to the point of preventing me from moving forward.
It would be comfortable and safe to remain here,
For this is where I feel safe and secure,
where my ability and confidence are not threatened.
But you are calling me to pass through
and enter into the unknown,
to put myself at risk, to tread the path that looks so
unsure, rambling, where I have to keep moving
because grass is everywhere underfoot.

Once I pass through I cannot turn back, because that gate
will have mysteriously disappeared from behind me.
Something holds me back.
My faith is shallow, my body frail.
You, Lord, are the perfect calling to the imperfect
to be your hands and voice.
The sins of the past hang around my neck
like a millstone, and you say to me;
go and do to others as I have done to you.
Forgive, love, serve, give, heal, preach, baptise.
You have given all for me,
you have trodden a more difficult path
on the way to the worst humankind can do to another.

Lord, there is a rightness about your calling,
for along with that invitation is a promise,
a promise that those who walk in the way of the Lord
will never travel alone.
You said, 'And surely I am with you always, to the very end
of the age.'
As I pass through the gate I know I am travelling
with a friend,
My God, my Father, guide me by your Holy Spirit
as I serve you
by serving others, bringing glory not to me, but to you.

L. W.

For you have been my help, and in the shadow of your wings I sing for joy. My soul clings to you; your right hand upholds me.

Psalm 63:17

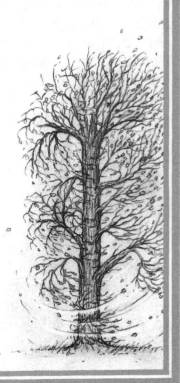

AUTUMN

Homeward Bound

Pauline Webb

As a daughter of the manse I never had a fixed abode. The seasons of my life were marked by the places I lived in. My first home was in a London suburb, where I was born. The springtime of my early childhood was spent in Leicestershire. Then came primary schooldays in Morecambe, where life often seemed like a summer seaside holiday. Next we moved to Shaw near Manchester, where, they say, it rains sometimes! As a teenager I lived in the Potteries and during my college years I lived at home in Hertfordshire. Adulthood brought me back into the London area, and I have lived in different parts of the metropolis ever since. So for me, now in the Autumn of my life, the word 'home' indicates but a resting-place on a journey. It has nothing to do with one particular location nor even with familiar furnishings.

In my childhood I was taught to treat both house and furniture with a distant respect, living in awe of circuit stewards who were the guardians of everything in the manse. In those days manses were fully furnished, often with the cast-offs of wealthier members of the congregation. It meant, as my mother used to say, that we had to develop a love of second-hand furniture and a capacity for plain living and high thinking. This prompted in me a parody of a well-known hymn:

Remember all the children
Who live within the manse
In lofty, barnlike buildings
And straitened circumstance.
The roof is caving inward,
There's lino on the floor,
But behind the peeling paintwork
Live the children of the poor.

Nevertheless 'home', wherever it was, was the place I always liked best. So what did the word really mean for me? I discovered its real meaning, after my first venture at running away from it. My parents were threatening to send me to boarding school, where many children of the manse went in those days in search of a more stable education. So I decided to run away. The escapade lasted only a few hours, for I soon became hungry, grubby and tired. Deciding to risk even the wrath I knew I would face from my anxious parents, I wearily turned back home. To my astonishment I was greeted with open arms, a warm bath and a good supper. It was only after I was tucked up in my clean, white bed that my parents made any reference to my wrongdoing and to the anxiety I had caused. Then in our prayers together they quoted the words of the children's hymn about that home where there is room for all who are 'washed and forgiven'.

So 'home' came to mean that place where we are welcomed, not because we deserve it, but because we are loved. It is that place where we can relax, be made clean from all the grubbiness of our lives, eat what we most enjoy and lay down the burdens of luggage we have carried with us on our journey. I remember, during my own most itinerant years working for the Methodist Missionary Society, one of my favourite songs was a Simon and Garfunkel lyric called 'Homeward Bound'. It expressed the feeling of sitting in a railway station, on the way to another 'gig' – in my case it was a 'deputation' preaching engagement – and, like the singer, I was just longing for the train to come and speed me back home again.

That longing for home persists through our whole lives. Even when those who made a home for us have passed on, or when we have chosen to leave the family home, we still need a home of our own. For over twenty years now I have lived alone, but 'home', my home, is as important to me as any family base. Despite the fact that no-one else lives with me, I still feel, as I turn the key in my door, that a welcome awaits me. I can put down whatever burden I've been carrying, make myself a cup of tea, and put up my feet. Often I can feel then an almost tangible presence of someone sharing my life with me. For those of us who live alone, meal times can be the loneliest times. I, for one, always welcome hospitality in other people's homes, but it is important to take the trouble to entertain guests in my own home at times. On the days when I am alone, I rarely succumb to the temptation not to bother to lay a tray or table as for a guest. As I pause to say grace, it is often then that I am most aware of the presence of the One who makes himself known in the breaking of bread.

The other times when I feel most conscious of sharing my life, even though I am alone, is at the beginning and ending of the day. One of the aspects of living alone that many people dread most is having no-one to talk things over with. So for me, prayer-time becomes an important time of conversation in which I can reflect on what has been happening, think through what lies ahead, and spend time quietly hearing what the Word of God has to say to me. I welcome all the aids to prayer and Bible study that come my way. It really helps to make the conversation two-way.

I have recently been much encouraged by discovering a book of Susanna Wesley's prayers. She did not find prayer easy, but she longed for those times when she could quietly talk over with God the things that concerned her most. Some of her prayers even read like arguments with the Deity! Many of them reflect all the pressures she was under. Far from living alone, she must have felt overcrowded at home for most of her life. In one of her prayers she expresses her longing for a quieter life, but she comes to a realistic acceptance of the fact that we have to make the most of whatever life we have, and she ends with the honest recognition that both bustle and quietness bring their temptations:

> Were I permitted to choose a state of life,
> or positively to ask of You
> anything in this world,
> I would humbly choose
> and beg that I might be placed in such a station
> where I might have daily bread with moderate
>   care,
> without so much hurry and distraction
> and that I might have more leisure
> to retire from the world without injuring my
>   dependants.

These are my present thoughts,
But yet I do not know whether such a state
would really be best for me.
Nor am I assured that if I had more leisure,
I should be more zealously devoted to You, my
    God,
and serve You better than now.
Perhaps there might be as many temptations
in a quiet and private life
as there are in this.

Susanna was right. Even the quietness and privacy of one's own home can become a temptation to complacency and selfishness. I never did like that line of the popular ballad which thanks God for 'those walls so firm and stout, keeping want and trouble out'. My own love of home should make me all the more sensitive to the needs of those who are the victims of one of the most tragic conditions of our time – homelessness. The very word strikes horror in my heart, and the only way I can assuage a sense of guilt at my own good fortune is to keep this 'Big Issue' (both literally and metaphorically) regularly in the forefront of my prayers and actions.

Nor should I ever think of my home now as my permanent resting-place. One advantage of a manse upbringing is that moving loses its terrors. I think I can face with equanimity the thought that one day I may have to give up this home for other, more sheltered housing. There may even come the day when I become so dependent on the help of others that I have to move into a residential Home. Such a prospect has seemed much less threatening to me since

I have visited the kinds of provision our Methodist Homes can offer to meet the various stages of our lives. I realise that I shall be fortunate if such provision is available when I need it. And even then there will be one more move ahead.

Jesus, who had no permanent home here on earth, has promised us that in his Father's home there are many rooms, and that he will be there when the time comes, waiting to welcome us home. There we shall lay down the baggage of our earthly lives, be washed clean of our grime and be reunited with all those we have loved. At last we shall find that fixed abode towards which all our lives we have been homeward bound.

Seed-time and harvest are separated in time, but inseparable in fact. Our Lord sowed without reaping, but the ages will reap the harvest. Spiritual work is done for eternity. Be patient in your husbandry.

Source unknown

Now every day the bracken browner grows,
  Even the purple stars
  Of clematis, that shone about the bars,
Grow browner; and the little autumn rose
  Dons, for her rosy gown,
  Sad weeds of brown.

Now falls the eve; and ere the morning sun,
  Many a flower her sweet life will have lost,
  Slain by the bitter frost,
Who slays the butterflies also, one by one,
  The tiny beasts
  That go about their business and their feasts.

Mary Coleridge, September

When saving for old age, be sure to put away a few pleasant thoughts.

Anonymous

It matters little where we pass the remnants of our days. A few more moons; a few more winters – and not one of the descendants of the mighty host that once moved over this broad land or lived in happy homes, protected by the Great Spirit, will remain to mourn over the graves of a people once more powerful and hopeful than yours. But why would I mourn at the untimely fate of my people? Tribe follows tribe, and nation follows nation, like the waves of the sea. It is the order of nature. The time of decay may be distant, but it surely comes for everyone. No one is exempt from the common destiny. So, we may be brothers (and sisters) after all. We shall see.

Chief Seattle, surrendering tribal lands
to the US government, 1854

Fix thou our steps, O Lord, that we stagger not at the uneven motions of the world, but steadily go on to our glorious home; neither censuring our journey by the weather we meet with, nor turning out of the way for anything that befalls us. The winds are often rough, and our own weight presses us downwards. Reach forth, O Lord, thy hand, thy saving hand, and speedily deliver us. Teach us, O Lord, to use this transitory life as pilgrims returning to their beloved home; that we may take what our journey requires, and not think of settling in a foreign country.

John Wesley

In the downhill of life, when I find I'm declining,
  May my lot no less fortunate be
Than a snug elbow-chair can afford for reclining,
  And a cot that o'erlooks the wide sea;
With an ambling pad-pony to pace o'er the lawn,
  While I carol away idle sorrow,
And blithe as the lark that each day hails the dawn
  Look forward with hope for tomorrow.

With a porch at my door, both for shelter and shade too,
  As the sunshine or rain may prevail;
And a small spot of ground for the use of the spade too,
  With a barn for the use of the flail;
A cow for my dairy, a dog for my game,
  And a purse when a friend wants to borrow;
I'll envy no nabob his riches or fame,
  Nor what honours await him tomorrow.

From the bleak northern blast may my cot be completely
　　Secured by a neighbouring hill;
And at night may repose steal upon me more sweetly
　　By the sound of a murmuring rill:
And while peace and plenty I find at my board,
　　With a heart free from sickness and sorrow,
With my friends may I share what today may afford,
　　And let them spread the table tomorrow.

And when I at last must throw off this frail covering
　　Which I've worn for threescore years and ten,
On the brink of the grave I'll not seek to keep hovering,
　　Nor my thread wish to spin o'er again:
But my face in the glass I'll serenely survey,
　　And with smiles count each wrinkle and furrow;
As this old worn-out stuff, which is threadbare today,
　　May become everlasting tomorrow.

John Collins

I believed the Word. I rested on it and practised it. I 'took God at his Word'. A stranger, a foreigner in England, I knew seven languages and might have used them perhaps as a means of remunerative employment, but I had consecrated myself to labour for the Lord. I put my reliance in the God who has promised, and he has acted according to his word. I've lacked nothing – nothing. I have had my trials, my difficulties, and my empty purse, but my receipts have aggregated tens of thousands of dollars, while the work has gone on these fifty-one years. Then with regard to my pastoral work for the past fifty-one years, I have had great difficulties, great trials and perplexities. There will always be difficulties, always trials. But God has sustained me under them and delivered me out of them, and the work has gone on.

George Muller, at the age of 76

If I did not simply live from one moment to the next, it would be impossible for me to keep my patience. I can see only the present, I forget the past and I take good care not to think about the future. We get discouraged and feel despair because we brood about the past and the future. It is such folly to pass one's time fretting, instead of resting quietly on the heart of Jesus.

Thérèse of Lisieux

Youth: Living, Dying and Asking: 'Dear God – why?'

Frank Topping

The bustle of Famagusta is behind us. We are in the country now. Ahead is the village of Paralimni. We can see the orange-groves and the vines and the occasional carob tree. Here and there isolated eucalyptus trees cast dappled patches of shade. It is hot, in the eighties. A woman, black dress, black headscarf, heavy shoes, is leading a donkey along the edge of an orange-grove. The trucks, RAF uniforms, everything, is covered in dust. It's in our hair, our mouths and eyes. Even the trees and the bushes blend with the pastel coloured earth and bleached rocks. The buildings rise up out of the earth like rectangular stones. Black holes in white walls are windows into cool interiors. In the street a woman is working a cement mixer. Old men with grizzled moustaches sit in groups outside doorways and children are playing, shouting. There is a donkey crossing the street. We slow down. 'What the hell was that! A bomb? A machine gun? God, the noise! Did someone scream?' Stop truck. It's Alan! Oh God, there's blood on the windscreen. He's hit. He's slithered down into the cab through the observation hole in the cab roof. Why is everybody shouting? 'Don't be stupid! Fire at what? You can't open fire on a street full of old men and children!' 'I don't know. I didn't see anything. It must have come from . . .' 'Shut up! We've got to get him into the back of the truck.' 'No, you don't have to be careful, he's dead. What . . . Because I just know he is, that's all.' A Greener police gun, lying on the ground beside a hole in a wall. Large shell full of lead shot. No need to aim, just point and . . .

'He was married, you know.'

'Yes.'

'Got kids. Did he say anything?'

He just said, "They've got me", sort of – surprised.'

They call us the Wild Men of Greco. Men are threatened, 'Watch it, or you'll get posted to Greco!' Cape Greco is about seven miles from Paralimni. There isn't a proper road, so the trucks make a lot of dust. No fresh water. My first meal here was six Rowntrees clear gums, two slices of Spam, a bar of chocolate and a tangerine.

They sent us dehydrated rations, but there is no fresh water. We bring the water in bowsers, tanker trucks, from Ayios Nikolaos, unless General Grivas's lads shoot holes in them. Fresh water is rationed for drinking and cooking purposes only. We wash our clothes in the sea, and swim a lot. We've been given bars of soap that are supposed to lather in salt water. They don't. A kind of scum forms, that's all. We shower and shave when we can get to Ayios Nikolaos; in between shaves we grow stubble and look like Humphrey Bogart in *The African Queen*. Clothes washed in salt water go sticky, then stiff, then disintegrate. Free order of dress, wear what you like. We look like bandits. When we drive into Ayios Nikolaos, the blancoed RAF police scowl, groan and make a show of shuddering.

The Army used to guard the camp, but there was too much friction between the Artillery and the dishevelled Brylcreem boys. It's first light. I've been on guard duty all night, just been relieved. I've clambered down to the water's edge, over the rocks beyond the lighthouse. There's a pale sky with a white line along the horizon. Nothing in sight, just sea and sky. I can see a bird, a big one. Wonder what it is? An eagle? It appears to be gliding along the horizon, except that it is only a few hundred yards away. The sky is getting brighter and the bird banks away towards the east, lifting, soaring, and suddenly, there they are, the mountains! The Syrian mountains! Absolutely as clear as crystal. Gradually the sky gets lighter and the mountains begin to fade, then the sun blips on to the horizon and the mountains have gone. A mirage of some sort, like a dream, like the dream I'm living now, waiting for the sun to blip on to the horizon when this whole island will disappear and I'll find myself awake and at home.

Escort duty. Stand on the passenger seat, like Alan, top half of my body through the circular hole in the cab roof, waiting for the bang. Waiting here, that's worse. Waiting for the gate to open and the trucks to rumble out. It's all right once you're on the road. If your number is on it, well that's that, nothing you can do about it, in fact it's exciting. It's the waiting in the camp that is almost unbearable. It's like diving off a high diving board; once you've gone it's all right, it's standing on the edge that's terrifying.

Two Turkish Cypriot boys, about fifteen or sixteen, are in the camp, being held in some kind of detention. By candlelight in our tent they are teaching us to sing 'Uskudari', in Turkish, and we are drinking Cypriot wine. Strange how it all has the same flavour, wine or spirits, I think it's the Retsina.

Williamson – his father is Henry Williamson who wrote *Tarka the Otter* – has organised a short-story writing competition. I'm producing a pantomime for Christmas; it's called *Like It or Lump It*. I wanted a stage and the discip. sergeant has built one out of concrete! Wonder where he got the cement from?

Another ambush, Paralimni again. In my tent I was shivering, shaking. Fear or the effects of sunburn, or both. Blisters on my back, like inflated tennis balls. MO says people of my colouring and skin shouldn't live here! Who's arguing? Swim with my shirt on in future. The trouble is you can't hit back, not with ambushes in the street. You just have to take it and lick your wounds. The word is, if someone does something suspicious, shoot him first. A boy shouted to me in Paralimni and then threw something. I suppose I should have shot him. I didn't. I caught what he had thrown; it was a pomegranate. If I had shot him it would have destroyed me. Somebody ran amok the other day in the camp, firing a sten gun all over the place. I think I know how he feels. I felt very bad the night after the pomegranate, couldn't sleep, and it wasn't the blisters. When I did sleep, it was worse. I was in a hole, like a well, hanging from the edge. The hole fell away beneath me for ever. I couldn't get a foothold and my fingers were losing their grasp and suddenly I was falling, down and down with that awful sensation in the stomach, and then I woke up on the floor. Hang on! Cling on! That's what I've got to do. But why? What for? What's so good about living like this? Sweating, shivering, shaking, being afraid. I do have the means of oblivion, just a squeeze on the trigger and no more anxiety, no more fear, oblivion. Or would it be like that? Oblivion or an eternity of shooting at laughing boys throwing pomegranates. Dear God, what is it all for?

The 'Big Blow' came last week. It was early and we weren't ready. Apparently the weather didn't obey the rule-book and, as everybody knows, the military live by the book. We were supposed to have dug trenches around the tents before the weather changed, but we hadn't even started when the storm hit us. I woke up suddenly. I didn't just stir, I was wide awake and alert. I could see the sky through the ventilation hole in the tent. The flysheet had gone and the tent poles were swaying. A rope outside was lashing the side walls.

There were three of us to a tent, all Merseysiders in ours, Derek, Geoff and me. I shook Derek and shouted, 'Derek! The tent's going!' I called to Geoff and rushed out of the tent. Outside a weird and ghostly 'Dance Macabre' was in progress. Shadowy figures were leaping about, shouts and wails swallowed in the wind. There was an eerie light that disappeared from time to time as clouds scudded across the face of the moon. A large cardboard box came bouncing towards me and then lifted in the air. I didn't see where it went. I saw our flysheet stretched out along the ground, flapping and straining against one remaining peg. I flung myself on top of it as Derek emerged from the tent. 'Quick!' I shouted. 'Get some rocks to hold this down!' We secured the flysheet as best as we could and turned our attention to the tent. Then the rain came.

Our line of tents stood at the foot of a steep and rocky hill. It was probably the protection of this hill that saved our tent. Others, further away, had been flattened, ripped, torn out by the roots. The rain was torrential but the wind did not ease off. Rivulets and streams began to run down the hillside. Like children on a beach, we attempted to channel the stream around the tents, making dams, diverting streams, digging with anything we could lay our hands on, tin plates, bits of wood.

'Where the hell is Geoff?'

'The begger's still in bed!'

We spent the whole night trying to secure the tent, piling rocks on to tent pegs and ropes and every now and then screaming at Geoff to get up, but he did not even stir. Perhaps he's been on the booze. He was always a heavy sleeper but this was ridiculous. Nothing would wake him, neither thunder, lightning, nor torrential rain or our loudest and foulest insults. We began to wonder if he had died.

In the morning the camp looked like a battlefield, tents down, some missing altogether; beds standing in strange isolation, the whole area strewn with the wreckage and debris of the storm. The great cook-house tent, an enormous marquee, had gone, blown into the sea. And there was Geoff, rubbing his eyes and asking, 'What's happened?'

Suddenly it's England, green, green, incredibly green England.

Demobbed, it was good to get home, to listen to my mother's stories, go to Mass, meet the family. Nothing seemed to have changed, except me. I felt removed from reality, everything was happening around me but I did not feel part of it, I felt like an observer, an outsider. To my amazement, I realised that I was homesick. The realisation filled me with horror. I was missing the camaraderie of men on active service. I was missing the trucks and my sten gun, the awful food, the feeling of being on the edge of danger and the daily possibility of deadly adventure. God knows, I'd been a reluctant warrior, but now, in my twenties, I was a retired veteran and I felt that I had lost something. Or could it be that I had found something? A sense of proportion? A realisation that life was too short to waste, and short or long, fullness depended on meaning and purpose and a certain amount of intensity, a sense of adventure to give it quality? One did not need to risk one's life for a doubtful cause, but the element of risk seems to be a necessary ingredient to being fully alive. Thank God I was home, but I was not home to hibernate, that was very clear. I did not intend to wake up in forty years' time, rubbing my eyes and asking, 'What's happened?'

'Another cup of tea love?' My mother waved towards the eternal teapot. 'It's fresh.'

'Hmm?'

'Another cup of tea?'

'Pardon?'

'A cup of tea – and a penny?'

'A penny? What's the penny for?'

'For your thoughts – Son.'

Thou seest my feebleness;
Jesus, be thou my power,
My help and refuge in distress,
My fortress and my tower.

Give me to trust in thee,
Be thou my sure abode,
My horn, and rock, and buckler be,
My Saviour and my God.

Myself I cannot save,
Myself I cannot keep;
But strength in thee I surely have,
Whose eyelids never sleep.

Charles Wesley

When, as a child, I laughed and wept, time crept.
When, as a youth, I dreamed and talked, time walked.
When I became a full-grown man, time ran.
And later, as I older grew, time flew.
Soon I shall find, while travelling on, time gone.
Will Christ have saved my soul by then?

Words on a clock in Chester Cathedral

Lord, thou knowest better than I know myself that I am growing older, and will some day be old.

Keep me from getting talkative, and particularly from the fatal habit of thinking that I must say something on every subject and on every occasion.

Release me from craving to straighten out everybody's affairs.

Keep my mind from the recital of endless details – give me wings to come to the point.

I ask for grace enough to listen to the tales of others' pains. Help me to endure them with patience.

But seal my lips on my own aches and pains – they are increasing, and my love of rehearsing them is becoming sweeter as the years go by.

Teach me the glorious lesson that occasionally it is possible that I may be mistaken.

Keep me reasonably sweet. I do not want to be a saint – some of them are so hard to live with – but a sour old woman is one of the crowning works of the devil.

Make me thoughtful – but not moody; helpful, but not bossy. With my vast store of wisdom it seems a pity not to use it all, but thou knowest, Lord, that I want a few friends at the end.

A Mother Superior's Prayer
(Anonymous)

He looks younger every day; and yet not with the same kind of youth he had before his back was bowed with the Chancellorship. 'Tis a more composed, chastened sort of rejuvenescence; rather the soft warmth of autumn, which sometimes seems more like May, than May itself: the enkindling, within this mortal tabernacle, of a heavenly Light that never grows dim, because it is immortal, and burns the same yesterday, today and for ever; a youthfulness of soul and mind characterised by growth; something with which this world and its fleeting fancies has nothing to do; something that a King can neither impart nor take away.

Margaret Roper (née More), speaking of her father, Sir Thomas More

Our life's a flying shadow, God the pole,
The needle pointing to him is our soul.

Inscription in Glasgow Cathedral

Grant unto us, Almighty God, that when our vision fails, and our understanding is darkened; when the ways of life seem hard, and the brightness of life is gone, to us grant the wisdom that deepens faith when the sight is dim, and enlarges trust when the understanding is not clear.

George Dawson

The feathers of the willow
Are half of them grown yellow
Above the swelling stream;
And ragged are the bushes,
And rusty now the rushes,
And wild the clouded gleam.

The thistle now is older,
His stalk begins to moulder,
His head is white as snow;
The branches all are barer,
The linnet's song is rarer,
The robin pipeth now.

R. Watson Dixon

O merciful God, heavenly Father, whether we sleep or wake, live or die, we are always thine. Wherefore I beseech thee heartily that thou wilt vouchsafe to take care and charge of me, that I may always be found to walk and live after thy will and pleasure, through Jesus Christ our Lord and Saviour.

Prayer Book of Queen Elizabeth I

The Darkness of God

Brenda Woods

The trouble with Christianity is that Christians are often portrayed as being happy people with no problems in their life. 'Keep your eyes fixed on Jesus and all will be well' intone those who live on the mountain tops, with scant regard for the rest of us whose lives seem to plummet into the valleys at the first opportunity. Yet where is faith to grow if not, like all seeds, in the darkness? And where will the voice of God be heard if not in the silence of the heart? Darkness and silence are rare commodities in the brash busyness of life, of work and church and church and work. Darkness can creep up on us, imperceptibly like the dusk, and suddenly we realise we can no longer see. As time goes by, our eyes become accustomed to the dark and our hearing to the silence and we begin to perceive new and strange shapes and sounds and to learn a new language, the language of God.

A lifetime of active service! Twenty years at the chalk face, time for God in a mission school in Southern Rhodesia, a comprehensive school in Battersea, buy a flat, teach in a Sunday school in Brixton, become involved at Hinde Street Methodist Church in central London, chair the Mission Committee, Class Leader, Pastoral Committee, Church Council, Head of Science, buy a house, decide to get married, decide not to get married, senior teacher with responsibility for Primary

Liaison, new curriculum initiatives, a government that begins to move the goal posts, work in the evenings, work at weekends, work, work, work. Don't sleep for a week at Christmas. Cry for another week in January. The awful realisation dawns . . . something is wrong. Seriously wrong. The darkness has descended. The world has fallen apart. Nothing remains. Everything is meaningless. The pain is often too much to bear. The pain of a ten-year relationship that is fizzling out, an inevitable end that only adds to the unbearable nature of everything. No solace at work, save in the filling of empty days. And God? Where now is God? This God whom I have served and worshipped all my life, and left secure at church, where is this God? Now, now I need you, need your comfort, consolation, presence. There is no God. There is only silence and darkness.

Days turn into weeks and weeks become months. The agony continues. I stand on the edge of the abyss and cling to nothing in order to avoid sinking into what seems to be even greater darkness. I have not yet learnt that one must go through such experiences, that there is no way forward that is not also down and through. Luckily for me, the minister has done a counselling course. He knows about such things and is prepared to walk beside me, to encourage me to begin to unclench my fists and let go into the dark. He lends me books. Books I never knew existed where I find myself described, where authors write of the journey to the centre, and the God whose seeming absence is his presence, and T. S. Eliot, whose *Four Quartets* speak to my soul of the darkness of God.

Gentle counselling begins to unlock the past. The wounds of childhood are far from healed, tears are in abundance. I return to school after a week away and a colleague in another department greets me with such warmth and 'How are you? We've all been so worried about you.' Worried about me? Why should she be? My absence surely has not affected her. It is the first time in my life that I have been conscious of being important to someone because of who I am and not for what I do. It is the most healing realisation of my life. The perfectionist who all her life has found fulfilment in achievement has for the first time found acceptance and love for who she is.

Summer comes. Nothing has changed, except I know I do not want to be a deputy head. But I do not know what I do want. Shall I sell up and buy a tea shop? No, everyone wants tea when the sun is shining. Or how about selling wild flower plants? The vision of twenty thousand little plants in pots at fifty pence a time is overwhelming. Would Wandsworth Common be able to contain them all? No, this is not for me. Wait. There is still no God, only silence and darkness. Wait.

An idea, a daft idea, hovers round the back of my head. I ignore it. It will not go away. I look at it with incredulity, I laugh at it. It will not go away. I tell myself I do not want to do that. I cannot do that. It is a very silly idea. It will not go away. It is the last Sunday before our minister moves on. In desperation I ask to see him after the service. We sit in his office. How can I tell him? His son comes in: 'Mummy says when are you coming home for lunch?' 'Soon.' As soon as I've told you about this very silly idea for which I cannot find the words. Embarrassed, I eventually mumble about God wanting me to be a minister and how daft this is and please will he tell me to go away and then perhaps this idea will go away and I'll be left in peace. He smiles, laughs and says it sounds authentic and I should go for it.

Tea shops and plants in pots suddenly seem very alluring. At least they do not require you to believe in anything much. But ministry? Surely a basic requisite might reasonably be assumed to be a strong faith, or at least a faith, some small mustard seed-like amount of faith. But all I do is weep and read books about the absence of God. Go for it? Well, why not? And so the first small step of faith is taken.

Local preachers' studies are tackled with the same degree of workaholic perfectionism as the rest of life. Physical illness results and months of hospital tests for some mystery tumour result in nothing. By now I have discovered retreats and retreat houses and spiritual direction and silence. I have discovered that God is a God of surprises, who delights in playing hide-and-seek, whose presence is elusive and delicious, who remains a mystery and yet comes unexpected and unbidden tangibly to enfold me in love. I am being taught that God's love is all I need, that God cannot be contained, that he must be sought after and yearned for, that his presence is pure gift. That the darkness is indeed 'the light, and the stillness the dancing'.*

I invest in a psychotherapist and I'm devastated by his death a few months later, just before the candidates' exams. Reluctantly I find another therapist and discover my reluctance is in the fact that she is a she.

118

Another deeply held belief is brought into the cruel light of day: can a woman be trusted to be good enough? Candidating for the ministry continually forces me to face the question: 'Why do you want to be a Methodist minister?' I usually reply that I don't! But I am passionately interested in three things – worship, pastoral care and spirituality – and I'm willing to leave it for others to decide whether ministry is the best way. 'They' decide it is and I'm off for two years to Wesley House theological college and then to spend a third year in Chicago to train as a spiritual companion.

Throughout these past few years I have struggled with depression, delved deeper into myself, continually questioned and wrestled with God and continued to meet him in unexpected places. One of the great lessons which God seems determined I should learn is that he is not to be contained by me, nor controlled by me. Drawn as I am to greater silence and contemplation, times of prayer are often empty or a struggle, and then God appears unsought as I walk by the river.

I remember the film *The Small Woman*, in which Gladys Aylward massages the feet of women and girls when, for the first time, they are unbound. The tears flow, for as life returns the pain is excruciating. The pain has been sometimes unbearable as others have helped life to flow again in parts of me that have been long bound. I thank God that there have been those with love and patience enough to stand alongside me and enable me to make the journey to the centre.

* T. S. Eliot, *The Four Quartets*

Say not the struggle nought availeth,
  The labour and the wounds are vain,
The enemy faints not, nor faileth,
  And as things have been, things remain.

If hopes were dupes, fears may be liars;
  It may be, in yon smoke concealed,
Your comrades chase e'en now the fliers,
  And, but for you, possess the field.

For while the tired waves, vainly breaking,
  Seem here no painful inch to gain,
Far back through creeks and inlets making
  Came, silent, flooding in, the main,

And not by eastern windows only,
  When daylight comes, comes in the light,
In front the sun climbs slow, how slowly,
  But westward, look, the land is bright.

                                    Arthur Hugh Clough

This seems a cheerless world, Donatus, when I view it from this fair garden under the shadow of these vines. But if I climbed some great mountain and looked out over wide lands, you know very well what I would see. Brigands on the high road, pirates on the seas . . . men murdered . . . Under all roofs, misery and selfishness. It is really a bad world, Donatus, yet in the midst of it I have found a quiet and holy people. They have discovered a joy which is a thousand times better than any pleasure of this sinful life. They are despised and persecuted, but they care not. They have overcome the world. These people, Donatus, are the Christians.

Cyprian, Bishop of Carthage,
in a letter dated AD 258

Give to the winds thy fears;
  Hope and be undismayed:
God hears thy sighs, and counts thy tears,
  God shall lift up thy head.

Through waves, and clouds, and storms
  He gently clears thy way:
Wait thou his time; so shall this night
  Soon end in joyous day.

Paul Gerhardt,
translated by John Wesley

Thank God, that I have lived to witness a day in which England is willing to give twenty millions sterling for the Abolition of Slavery.

William Wilberforce

The Israelites were always complaining. When they were fed up with the endless trekking through the desert, oh how much better they reckoned it had been back in Eygpt; but then it's always tempting, when our lives are going through a desert patch, to look fondly at what we kid ourselves were the *good old days*. Selective memories deceive us. Even the weather was better years ago – wasn't it?

No. Even if you had a guiding pillar of smoke, there'd always be someone moaning that the fire needed making up or the ashes raking out. But moaning's no help. What the past says, if we're honest, is that we've come to where we are through days that have had their ups and downs, their struggles and dull patches, as well as moments of pleasure and joy and achievement, and it's silly to expect the present to be any different. And that's not being gloomy. It's just being realistic. It's saying there's every chance the days ahead will have good times to offset the bad, sunshine as well as rain . . . It's often an uncomfortable mixture, but the working together of pain and pleasure into something that is ultimately good beyond our wildest dreams, is the only vision that makes sense of life.

Richard Adams,
Visions and Voices

Where is it written that ageing is a battle? Where did we get the idea that growing older was something to be avoided at all costs? Who decided that young was beautiful and anything older than young was unacceptable? When did age become a liability?

Is it some kind of superplot hatched up by cosmetic company owners and model agencies? In a society whose fastest growing population segment is over forty, we seem to have put the cart before the horse, so to speak. Instead of emphasising the mature look, the beauty of an older face, the comforting curves of a less-than-lean body, we insist that we all become Peter Pans and refuse to grow up or grow older. Age is no longer a factor of value, but a secret that must be hidden at all costs. We are a society which believes that, unlike fine wine or precious antiques, our value decreases with age.

I don't really like growing older, mind you. I resent the inability of my body to bounce back from a late night, and I find it difficult to accept my increasing aches and pains. Where I used to work cheerfully in the garden all day, I now have to pace myself or suffer backache as a consequence. I don't like being told by a doctor who is still wearing braces on his teeth, 'You're not getting any younger, you know,' and I don't like having to remember to take my vitamins in the winter and put on my sunscreen in the summer. Getting older seems to mean more and more maintenance of the general body plant.

I'm glad that my spiritual body is a lot easier to maintain. In fact, it becomes stronger each day that I walk with the Lord. Unlike my earthly shell that reaches a peak and then slides inexorably downhill, my spiritual body continues ever onward and upward. As I use my spiritual gifts, I can feel them strengthen and sustain me. My faith deepens; my hope grows; my peace abides. The spiritual body thrives on daily use.

And the view just gets better and better on the upward journey!

Patricia Wilson,
*How Can I Be Over The Hill
When I Haven't Seen The Top Yet?*

Let not the eyes grow dim, look not backward but forward; the soul must uphold itself like the sun. Let us labour to make the heart grow larger as we become older, as the spreading oak gives more shelter.

Richard Jeffries

The Death in the Desert

Caroline Cox

There are times in any person's life when the 'seasons' can change very abruptly – when black thunderclouds of impending storms suddenly darken a sun-filled sky and when danger or death may loom near. As the Bible puts it: 'In the midst of life we are in death.'

I would like to tell a story about such a change – from moments of relative security and comfort to fear and the danger of imminent death. The story also illustrates another kind of change: the adjustment to the relative freedom (or emptiness) which comes when children leave home and there are no longer the responsibilities of caring for a busy, bustling family.

After our youngest departed, I accepted an urgent invitation to work as a nurse in remote areas in Northern Sudan, in response to a crisis caused by an acute shortage of nurses, which was threatening to close key health care projects. The organisation for which I was working, Emmanuel International (or Fellowship for African Relief as it is known in Sudan) adopted the principle that its volunteers did not go to people and simply hand out Western medicines; instead we lived with the local people, alongside them, to establish trust based on friendship, before developing a health care programme.

126

When I arrived in Khartoum, the local organisers must have thought I was either a tough old bird, or dispensable, or both. For they sent me to work on their toughest project – developing an Immunisation Programme in a remote desert area of North Kordofan. Thus, I set off with Katherine, a Canadian nurse colleague, for a remote little township called Hamrat El Wiz, in the midst of the desert due west of Khartoum. We lived in a compound with no electricity or running water – and, rather frighteningly, no radio contact with the wider world.

The local community made us welcome with the hospitality characteristic of the Sudanese people. After a few weeks, we had completed our local health programme in Hamrat, and ventured further afield, to even more remote settlements. This often landed us in tricky situations. On one such occasion our jeep broke down in the middle of the desert, and we nearly came to a nasty end, that of dying of thirst. We had to try to walk to our destination, but it proved too far away.

We were rescued by a boy who had been tending goats in a wadi (a dried-up river bed) who found us and guided us to his village. The local people treated us with great kindness, killing a goat in our honour (no time to be sentimental: the goat was a great act of generosity from a poor community on the edge of famine). On that occasion, we were able to make it back to Hamrat courtesy of the local camel. A more randy animal is hard to imagine, but we clung on for six hours and survived to tell the tale!

But this story begins on the day that we set out for a far more remote location, a small village called Mahbis. The desert is so remote that there are no maps, roads, no tracks, no other vehicles. You just drive by the sun, asking passing Arabs on camels for direction. We drove for several hours, and passed a little settlement and enquired the way. The Arabic word 'Tawali' denotes distance – the longer, the further – and the 'Tawali' was still disconcertingly long! We continued, nevertheless, despite the roughness of the terrain and the need to negotiate several deep and dangerous wadis. In each, our Land Rover nearly got bogged down in the soft sand of the dried river bed, and had great difficulty in clawing its way up the steep banks, using all the power of the bottom gear of the low ratio gear box.

Our interpreter, Sami, was driving at the time and put his foot on the accelerator – hard. We bounced over a relatively flat part of desert for a few minutes at 100 kilometres an hour, until disaster struck and we hit a rock. The Land Rover nearly somersaulted; everything inside did. We were bruised but not badly hurt. But all our water containers burst open and we lost all our drinking water – a serious matter in the midst of the desert, with temperatures of forty degrees. There was no option except to turn round to try to make it back to Hamrat. Then our hearts sank: the engine started, but the wheels would not move. The impact had damaged the clutch. We set about trying to repair the damage, when darkness fell.

Suddenly, out of the gathering twilight, an Arab appeared on a camel. My first words, in my survival

Arabic, were an anxious plea: 'Is there water in this wadi?' Mercifully there was – although we had to dig for it. It was filthy and full of indescribable objects. But there was scrub wood, so we lit a fire, boiled the water and settled down to sleep on the sand, comforted by the fact that at least we need not die of thirst.

In the morning, at first light, we took it in turns to try to mend the Land Rover and to boil water, in preparation for the inevitable thirst and dehydration which come as sun and temperatures rise. After two hours' work on the vehicle, we reassembled it, and, holding our breath, tried to see if it would work. The engine turned over encouragingly – but the wheels remained obstinately immobile.

I turned back to boiling more water, and took the opportunity to say my morning prayers. I had a prayer book which combined daily prayers with psalms and poems. When I read the poetry selection for the day, my heart stood still: there was an extract from T. S. Eliot's play, *Murder in the Cathedral*, with the words leaping off the page: 'THE DEATH IN THE DESERT'. I felt a shock-horror chill run down my spine, and asked God if he was giving me a message! In any event, I felt it was not one to share with my colleagues, Katherine and Sami.

I returned to my task of boiling water, decided I could see no way out of this pickle, and pondered on Christ's prayer in the Garden of Gethsemane.

Ten minutes later I suddenly heard the Land Rover moving. Sami had also been praying and had the inspiration of trying to start in the high ratio of gears. It would go. But we were then faced with an agonising dilemma: should we try the return journey, relying on high ratio gears and running the risk of getting stuck in one of those steep wadis with no water and ending up as a pile of white bones in the desert? Or should we stay where we knew there was water, but with little hope of rescue – at least for the many weeks it would take to get a message by one of the infrequent 'souk' or market trucks plying between Hamrat and Khartoum; then waiting for a relief vehicle to reach Hamrat, then wondering if it would ever find us – many miles away and with all tracks in the sand long since blown away?

We prayed. And we decided to try to return to Hamrat. We also prayed every time we reached one of those dreaded wadis – and each time, as we drove into the dried river bed, relying on high gears only to pull us out of the deadly soft sand, it felt as if an invisible hand plucked us out. The Land Rover almost floated across each potentially deadly wadi.

We arrived back in Hamrat with precision timing: just in time to address a meeting of local sheikhs which we had arranged before we left on that almost lethal journey.

The memories which remain are an unbounded admiration for the uncomplaining courage of my colleagues as we faced the possibility of death in the desert, and the salutary message, that, although God saw fit to rescue us on that occasion, we must be prepared to pray the Gethsemane prayer – and to pray for the courage to pray it. And that is an uncomfortable lesson which needs to be remembered, not only in bizarre situations like the deserts of Sudan, but in any place, at any time.

But I also learnt that it is only to the extent that we are prepared to pray that prayer that God's amazing saving power can work – not necessarily in physical rescue, but in spiritual gifts. I do not know how I would have responded if we had been put to the ultimate test. All I know now is that as a Christian, I must learn to trust in a God who has promised us that his grace is – and always will be – sufficient, through all the changing scenes of life.

As I grow old it seems that I
Grow old as grows the westward sky
When day is coming to its close:
For life takes on a tint of rose
I had not known in life's hot noon.
Now in the night that comes so soon
I see new stars I had not seen,
A surer faith, a peace serene,
As I grow old.

As I grow old the winds of life
Die down, the hate, the hurt, the strife.
The waters calm, the waves are still,
I want no triumph, wish no ill
To any man. Now from my heart
The ancient angers all depart.
New friends I know, new songs are sung,
New joys are mine – yes, I grow young
As I grow old.

Douglas Malloch

Thank God that as one reaches the autumn of life it is possible to recall life's precious moments.   Their memory quickens faith and deepens content, and permits us to hope that when the winter comes and the storms burst upon us, there may again be heard in the heart of the storm that still, small voice.

So I think, as in life's autumn I watch the autumn of Nature in all its beauty. For though the sun shines upon me as I write, and one of the fairest prospects in England stretches before me, I know the storms must soon come, and the leaves fast fall, and the snow shut us in on this hill-top. How shall I face the winter? One thing I will endeavour to do, I will hail it with content. It is not easy to grow old graciously, I know, but maybe I can grow old contentedly. And while the shadows lengthen – for the sun still shines – I can learn in this peaceful scene to be restful and hopeful. I have had my innings and enjoyed it, and if I have not carried my bat in glory, I have added one or two runs to the score of life, and have tried to play the game. It is now for me to gather up the fragments of life that nothing be lost; and, as the days shorten, to remember that there is life still left in the winter trees, and to use what life there is for the highest and noblest. I can still make George Frederick Watts' motto my own, 'The utmost for the highest'; and though the summer be past and the autumn ended, find in the winter that the best is yet to be.

Fairfields Whitwell,
The Hill of Contentment

The seas are quiet when the winds give o'er;
So calm are we when passions are no more.
For then we know how vain it was to boast
Of fleeting things, so certain to be lost.
Clouds of affection from our younger eyes
Conceal that emptiness which age descries.

The soul's dark cottage, batter'd and decay'd,
Lets in new light through chinks that Time
      hath made:
Stronger by weakness, wiser men become
As they draw near to their eternal home.
Leaving the old, both worlds at once they view
That stand upon the threshold of the new.

                    Edmund Waller, from *Last Verses*

If a thing is old, it is a sign that it was fit to live. Old families, old customs, old styles survive because they are fit to survive. The guarantee of continuity is quality. Submerge the good in a flood of the new, and the good will come back to join the good which the new brings with it. Old-fashioned hospitality, old-fashioned politeness, old-fashioned honour in business had qualities of survival. These will come back.

Anonymous

Eternity is crying out to you louder and louder as you near its brink. Rise, be doing; count your resources; learn what you are not fit for, and give up wishing for it; learn what you can do, and do it.

F. W. Robertson

With the passing of Queen Victoria, the great Victorian era ended. As we watched her funeral procession pass along the streets of London on January 22nd, 1901, a solemn hush seemed to fall upon the waiting crowd, and indeed upon the whole nation. It realised vaguely that it was the end of a great historic period and that we were entering upon a century which would bring to us unknown experiences. Little did we imagine all that would happen to us before that century was half over, and how the peaceful, happy years behind us were gone like a pleasant dream and that the world would soon be convulsed in a titanic struggle against the forces of evil.

Katherine Price Hughes,
The Story of My Life

Be patient with us, O God, as the day darkens, and suffer not our hearts to fail beneath the shadow of our sins and the remembrance of our offences. For with thee is forgiveness, and thy right hand is strong to uphold all them that put their trust in thee. Thine, O Lord, is the praise, who hast made us in thine own image and redeemed us by thy Son. Help us to open our hearts to the Saviour of the world, and to receive the Spirit whom he has sent.

Source unknown

There was once a very old man, whose eyes had become dim, his ears dull of hearing, his knees trembled, and when he sat at table he could hardly hold the spoon and spilt the broth upon the table-cloth or let it run out of his mouth. His son and his son's wife were disgusted at this, so the old grandfather at last had to sit in the corner behind the stove, and they gave him his food in an earthenware bowl, and not even enough of it. And he used to look towards the table with his eyes full of tears. Once, too, his trembling hands could not hold the bowl, and it fell to the ground and broke. The young wife scolded him, but he said nothing and only sighed. Then they bought him a wooden bowl for a few half-pence, out of which he had to eat.

They were sitting thus when the little grandson of four years old began to gather together some bits of wood upon the ground. 'What are you doing there?' asked the father. 'I am making a little trough,' answered the child, 'for father and mother to eat out of when I am big.' The man and his wife looked at each other for a while, and presently began to cry. Then they took the old grandfather to the table, and henceforth always let him eat with them, and likewise said nothing if he did spill a little of anything.

The brothers Grimm

Set Your Troubled Hearts at Rest

Timothy Dudley-Smith

'Set your troubled hearts at rest' –
hear again the word divine;
all our Father does is best;
let his peace be yours and mine.

Trusting still in God above,
set your troubled hearts at rest;
find within a Father's love
comfort for a soul distressed.

When you come to make request
know that God will answer prayer;
set your troubled hearts at rest,
safe within a Father's care.

Be at peace, then, and rejoice,
loved and comforted and blessed;
hear again the Saviour's voice:
'Set your troubled hearts at rest.'

My flesh and my heart may fail, but God is the strength of my heart and my portion forever.

Psalm 73:26

WINTER

Refusing to Retire

Bruce Kent

In a few months I will be sixty-seven years old. I can't believe it. At twenty-one I thought forty was well over the hump. At forty I thought sixty was the time for the Zimmer frame. Now, over sixty, I think that being old is dear Fenner Brockway and Philip Noel Baker in their nineties. Fenner nearly made his century but the Lord had other plans.

At least I have come to accept that I'm never going to be Prime Minister, Archbishop of Westminster, an expert hang-glider, or the first sixty-seven-year-old to get to the top of Mount Everest. Gradually one realises that a lot of far less impossible doors have finally closed. Life moves on. Other generations are on their way. They know all about the Internet, parliamentary procedure, the workings of the European Union, chess and classical music. They are coming up from behind and at sixty-seven you are getting in their way.

By most world standards sixty-seven is old indeed. Recently I picked up a leaflet which explained that if the world was a village of one thousand inhabitants only sixty would be over the age of sixty-five, and three-hundred-and-fifty would be children. When I look at the obituaries (which I do with more interest than before) I cannot fail to notice that I am older than many of those listed.

I even get a state pension, having paid the stamps for a long time – one of my few bits of sensible forward-planning.   Thanks to Ken Livingstone's Greater London Council, I travel free on tubes and buses. My hair is thinning from the back, so I don't see the bald patch in the mirror, though I can hardly fail to notice the colour. My problem is that I don't feel old. I don't want to be old. I refuse to retire as custom and convention demands.

Five years ago my wife and I went on one of those cheap pre-Christmas holidays to Majorca and I found myself in amongst a party of old people. In pastel-coloured track suits, refugees from the British winter, they went on outings, played games and had sing-songs. They were nice people, but I did not want to be one of them. Nevertheless I have to face facts. Young people even occasionally stand up for me on the tube. I'm introduced at meetings as the 'veteran' peace campaigner. Veteran? I don't like the word. There is a long way to go yet. So I resent my new classification but my head tells me that by any reasonable estimation I have had three-quarters of an interesting life. But what has been achieved by years of campaigning?

Such high hopes I had of Churches. Christianity, I believed and still believe, could hold up a different model of human relationships. Ours is a politics of equality, justice, non-violence, poverty, internation-alism and trusteeship. We ought to be one in the Body of Christ and trustees for God of all that we have: strangers and guests, not exploiters of the world which we have been given.

Of course I have my Christian heroes – Donald Soper, Trevor Huddleston, Dorothy Day, Helder Camara, and many others. But as institutions the Churches have not moved far. They are still much happier with remedial work than they are with challenges to the structures built by Caesar and to Caesar's ideas on security. For long years Church leaders, with a variety of qualifications and caveats, came down in the end on the side of the Government on issues of nuclear security. When, in the critical debates of the 1980s, we needed Church support, it was not there. Rarely were leadership voices even raised to defend fellow Christians, in CND and other peace and disarmament organisations, who were being showered with abuse and misrepresentation from Government circles.

Now, at last, Archbishop Martino, representing the Vatican at the UN, has rejected nuclear deterrence – the idea that peace can be built on threats to inflict barbaric punishments on innocent people far away. Said he: 'Maintaining nuclear detererrence into the twenty-first century will not aid but impede peace. Nuclear deterrence prevents genuine nuclear disarmament.'

I have had enough of Church statements. What I wanted was Church action in the form of practical help for the peace organisations which range from the Campaign Against the Arms Trade to the United Nations Association. It has not been forthcoming.

Long ago the Dutch bishops were right when they said that peace meant more than a pious wish in our hearts and on our lips. It means giving it a real place 'in our educational work, in our political convictions, in our faith, in our prayer, and in our budget'. Quakers apart, that kind of practical support for peace organisations has not been there. Could there not even have been some official Church reaction when the leader of the New Labour Party said late in 1995 that he was not only willing to press the nuclear button in retaliation, but would not exclude the possibility of doing so before anyone else? Yet anyone looking at a picture of devastated Hiroshima knows exactly what pressing the button means in dreadful, criminal reality.

Is this, therefore, a time for nostalgic disappointment? Has campaigning been a waste of time? The might-have-beens are all too obvious. If only the Churches had stood with Mikhail Gorbachev when, in the late eighties, a new Europe began to look possible. If only the Churches had come off the fence on nuclear deterrence and opposed nuclear escalation in clear terms. 'If only' is too pessimistic. It is to ignore so much that is positive that has happened. Change comes in ways and at times that we least expect. How few people, even experts, predicted the collapse of the Iron Curtain and the restructuring of Europe which took place in 1989. Citizens' protests and economic disaster brought down the barriers across Europe with a series of hammer blows.

Who would have guessed a few years ago that a determined group of internationally-minded individuals could actually work a complicated UN procedure so effectively that the World Court is now considering its advisory opinion on the legality of nuclear weapons and of nuclear deterrence. This has been a miracle of effective campaigning which has been opposed at every point by the governments of the nuclear powers.

Twenty years ago the great development organisations, ranging from Christian Aid to CAFOD, were unwilling to acknowledge, in their publicity, that the militarisation of the world is the greatest cause of world poverty. Who would have thought then that they would now be in the forefront of the campaign against landmines and willing in many ways to press to the limits their 'charitable' status?

It is true that massive problems remain. The horrors of the recent Balkan conflict remind us of the truth of Toynbee's claim that ninety per cent of the real religion of ninety per cent of the people is nationalism. We still have a long way to go before it really does not matter if one is labelled a Jew or Samaritan, and all nations gather at the holy mountain under the authority of God.

There are questions of a personal sort. If I had been more inclined to winning hearts rather than arguments would more minds have been changed? Would it have been better to work strenuously from within rather than without? I cannot say. Life is not a series of considered choices but for the most part hurried decisions on difficult paths with obscure signposts.

Regrets? Certainly, that I did not marry sooner. How differently I thought when first I was ordained. Celibacy divided the officers from the other ranks in God's army, and I was going to be an officer. What a long way from reality those arguments in favour of

compulsory celibacy seem to be now. There are of
course exceptional vocations to the single life. There
are some who carry the cross of having no choice. But
for most people the companionship and partnership of
marriage simply make common sense. Efforts to
maintain compulsory celibacy often damage the priest
concerned and not infrequently those with whom he
comes into contact.

There are other fences which I cannot mend. When I
was a child there were sometimes squabbles which led
to sulks, but sulks came to an end and we were all soon
friends again. But I am not a child now. There are
those with whom I have fallen out, to whom I will
never be reconciled in this world. I can pray for them
and think about them, but sometimes too many bridges
have been blown, too many hurts exchanged and too
many separate roads taken. That is a sadness to which
there is no answer.

But such regrets are balanced by so many positive
changes. Campaigning has not been a waste of time
but a privilege. Who could regret the friendships
made in the great freemasonry which joins all those
engaged in practical work for a better world. There
has been an ecumenism in common worship in the
open air outside military bases which has never been
experienced inside cathedrals.

Looking back, when I was young I must have been a
kind of Saul when it came to religion. Mine were the
days of the One True Church to which other
Christians, if they really were Christians, were tied by
invisible bonds whether they liked it or not. It was a

time when every question had its knock-down answer. From the Inquisition to Indulgences I knew exactly what to say. Loyalty to the Church and obedience to Authority were the major virtues. It was a religion of mathematical certainty rather than the religion of a journey in faith. Now it seems to me that the less dogmatic I become, the more God is part of my life. So at sixty-seven I look forward to many more lively decades yet and make my own the words on Winifred Holtby's tombstone: 'God give me work till my life shall end, and life until my work is done.'

The cross is always basic; it brings us back to the source of our new life. The sacrifice of Golgotha is our confidence that we are forgiven, that though our sins make us scarlet, we shall be as white as snow; and as far as the East is from the West, just that far will he remove our sins from us. *He died* and so we are freed of any illusion that we have to *be* anything or *do* anything in order to be loved and accepted of God.
He died, but more. 'I am alive for evermore,' Jesus said. 'I have the keys of Death and Hades.' The confirmation of new life is here in the resurrection: Jesus is alive for evermore, and we have his promise, 'Because I live, you will live also.'

Maxie Dunnam,
Jesus' Claims – Our Promises

That wise Being, who knows well how to extract good out of evil, has shown us one way of making this universal frailty highly conducive both to our virtue and happiness. Even grief, if it leads us to repentance, and proceeds from a serious sense of our faults, it is not to be repented of, since those who sow in tears shall reap in joy.

John Wesley

Saturday 12th [December 1801]. Snow upon the ground . . . All looked cheerful and bright. Helm Crag rose very bold and craggy, a Being by itself, and behind it was the large ridge of mountain, smooth as marble and snow white. All the mountains looked like solid stone, on our left, going from Grasmere, ie. White Moss and Nab Scar. The snow hid all the grass, and all signs of vegetation, and the rocks showed themselves boldly everywhere, and seemed more stony than rocks or stone. The birches on the crags beautiful, red brown and glittering. The ashes glittering spears with their upright stems.

Dorothy Wordsworth,
Grasmere Journal

Though I am dead grieve not for me with tears,
Think not of death with sorrowing and tears;
I am so near that every tear you shed touches and tortures me, though you think me dead.
But when you laugh and sing in glad delight, my soul is lifted upward to the light.
Laugh and be glad for all that life is giving and I, though dead, will share your joy in living.

Anonymous

Like as the thrush in winter, when the skies
Are drear and dark, and all the woods are bare,
Sings undismayed, till from his melodies
Odours of spring float through the frozen air –
So in my heart when sorrow's icy breath
Is bleak and bitter and its frost is strong;
Leaps up, defiant of despair and death
A sunlit fountain of triumphant song.
Sing on, sweet singer, till the violets come
And south winds blow, sing on prophetic bird!
O if my lips, which are for ever dumb
Could sing to men what my sad heart has heard
Life's darkest hour with songs of joy would ring,
Life's blackest frost would blossom into Spring.

Edmond Holmes

There is nothing in the world of which I feel so certain.
I have no idea what it will be like, and I am glad that I
have not, as I am sure it would be wrong. I do not
want it for myself as mere continuance, but I want it
for my understanding of life. And moreover 'God is
love' appears to me nonsense in view of the world he
has made, if there is no other.

William Temple,
speaking of eternal life

Part in peace: Christ's life was peace,
Let us live our life in him;
Part in peace: Christ's death was peace,
Let us die our death in him.

Part in peace: Christ's promise gave
Of a life beyond the grave,
Where all mortal partings cease;
Brothers, sisters, part in peace.

Sarah Flower Adams

Be of good comfort, Master Ridley, and play the man;
we shall this day light such a candle, by God's grace, in
England as I trust shall never be put out.

Hugh Latimer
(to Nicholas Ridley before they
were burned at the stake for heresy)

*Had we lived, I should have had a tale to tell of the
hardihood, endurance, and courage of my companions which
would have stirred the heart of every Englishman. These
rough notes and our dead bodies must tell the tale.*

Captain Robert Scott

Retirement

Ann Shepherdson

Is retirement a joy or burden for you?

Maybe you are preparing to retire, or you may have just entered upon this new way of life; or have you already adjusted to the new circumstances and situations it brings?

May I share with you the reactions of John and Linda? They had looked forward to retirement and planned for this new phase of their lives together. When it arrived they were ready to develop new interests and hobbies through which they found undiscovered talents. They enjoyed long holidays, exploring parts of the world they had only dreamed about. Some days of each week they spent with family and friends, enjoying the laughter, joy, pleasure and the delight of their company. They found happiness in caring for their beloved grandchildren. Life felt less burdensome, with fewer responsibilities. They felt free. Now they had time to decorate their home. Their neighbours commented on their professionalism and team spirit. John watched films and used his computer whilst Linda took pleasure in her gardening. They both felt that they had fulfilled their part in the working world and were now able to enjoy the fruits of their labour in this new season of their lives together. After the first flush of retirement they were now ready to give their time and expertise to various voluntary organisations such as the Heart Foundation and the Hospice movement.

Whereas Bill, looking at the state of the company, dreaded being made redundant because at his age it would mean retirement. When the axe fell, Bill and his wife Sarah were thrust into a new phase of living without time to plan or prepare. Bill missed his colleagues and the companionship which he'd taken for granted for so long. Bill and Sarah's world had shrunk and they felt out of touch. Following the loss of status, power, a good salary and therefore a good lifestyle, they mourned for all they had lost. The days and weeks seemed so empty and the time dragged for them both. Once Bill had been known by his trade and employment; he had been proud of his work, but now he felt vulnerable and isolated. He knew that his wife was deeply affected by his retirement. Sarah was no longer alone at home, or in charge of the domestic scene, and she had to change her lifestyle and routine to adapt to their new situation. A perceptive friend saw what was happening and challenged them to share and support one another and so find a way through this difficult period.

I am reminded of words from the book entitled *The Prophet* by Kahlil Gibran: 'But let there be spaces in your togetherness. And let the winds of heaven dance between you. And stand together yet not too near together; For the pillars of the temple stand apart. And the oak tree and cypress grow not in each other's shadow.'

Lastly, here is a glimpse of someone who lives alone. Mary felt that the transition from work to retirement was difficult and painful, but the telephone and letters were a lifeline which helped to dispel the loneliness. She visited family and friends in many parts of the country to renew and enjoy old relationships. Mary appreciated the freedom to follow her own interests, choose good holidays, and give her time and talents to the local church and other organisations, through which she ministered to Christ himself. There were also new opportunities to love and be loved, to mix with new groups of people and to reach out and care.

Retirement affected these three groups of people quite differently. It meant joy and fulfilment for Linda and John, frustration and disappointment for Sarah and Bill. After a period of adjustment, Mary accepted her situation and enjoyed it to the full.

All had so much to give, both of their experience and time. Thank God that they all, eventually, found contentment and satisfaction.

> *There is a time for everything,*
> *and a season for every activity under heaven:*
>
> *A time to be born,*
> *a time to be renewed.*
>
> *A time to work,*
> *a time to retire.*
>
> *A time to uproot,*
> *a time to plant.*

A time to give,
a time to receive.

A time to mix,
a time to be alone.

A time to cry,
a time to laugh.

A time for adventure,
a time for discovery.

A time to be still,
a time to grow.

What shall you do with the rest of your life? How will you use this gift of retirement?

Methodism was raised up to spread scriptural holiness. John Wesley encouraged people to experience the grace of Jesus Christ personally and grow in the knowledge and love of God. Therefore retirement enables people to have more time to pray, talk and listen, to study and reflect upon the Bible. Some may choose to attend retreats or Christian conferences, or to follow a pilgrimage. Others may come close to God through listening to music, and reading various types of books. Surely the aim of retirement is to use the time wisely, to acknowledge inner hurts and fears, to find wholeness and become holy.

My retired grandmother was a lovely person. We were the best of friends. I remember her as a generous and kind lady, with a warm smile and much love in her heart. I recall the quality of her life rather than what she said and did. Shall we be remembered by the way in which we love?

As Mother Teresa wrote: 'Holiness is not a luxury of the few but a simple duty for you and me, so let us be holy as our Father in heaven is holy.' And St Thomas said, 'Sanctity consists in nothing else but a firm resolve – the heroic act of a soul abandoning itself to God.' Our progress in holiness depends on God and on ourselves – on God's grace and on our willingness to be holy.

So let us continue to bear the fruits of justice, joy and tolerance, to name but a few qualities that touch many lives. Let us allow retirement to be a joyful experience through which we discover our identity as children of God. During this season of life we must come to know again, or for the first time, our worth measured by the manger, cross and empty tomb.

Dear Lord,
you have given us
the gift of retirement,
and so the time
in which to grow
into your likeness.
May your healing hands be upon us
to comfort, bless and make whole.
May your love fill our hearts,
that we may serve you with joy.
May your grace enable us to
walk the way of holiness,
loving you and our neighbours.

*May you guide our steps,
so that we may live by faith,
assured of your presence.
Bless us in our new phase of life.
Assured that we are children of God,
and in the joys
and sorrows of this time,
help us to know again
that we are precious and honoured
in your sight.
That our past, present and future
are safe in your
wounded hands of love.*

Glorious God, give me grace to amend my life, and to have an eye to my end without begrudging death, which to those who die in you, good Lord, is the gate of a wealthy life.

And give me, good Lord, a humble, lowly, quiet, peaceable, patient, charitable, kind, tender and pitiful mind, in all my words and all my thoughts.

Give me, good Lord, a full faith, a firm hope, and a fervent charity, a love of you incomparably above the love of myself.

Give me, good Lord, a longing to be with you, not to avoid the calamities of this world, not so much to attain the joys of heaven, as simply for love of you.

And give me, good Lord, your love and favour, which of my love of you, however great it might be, I could not deserve were it not for your great goodness.

These things, good Lord, that I may pray for, give me your grace to labour for.

Thomas More, written a week before his death

At the close of life the question is –
Not how much you have got,
But how much you have given.
Not how much you have won,
But how much you have done.
Not how much you have saved,
But how much you have sacrificed.
Not how much you were honoured,
But how much you have loved and served.

Anonymous

I have thought much lately of the possibility of my leaving you all and going home. I am come to that stage of my pilgrimage that is within sight of the River of Death, and I feel that now I must have all in readiness day and night for the messenger of the King. I have had sometimes in my sleep strange perceptions of a vivid spiritual life near to and with Christ, and multitudes of holy ones, and the joy of it is like no other joy – it cannot be told in the language of the world. What I have then I know with absolute certainty, yet it is so unlike and above anything we conceive of in this world that it is difficult to put into words. The inconceivable loveliness of Christ! It seems that about him there is a sphere where the enthusiasm of love is the calm habit of the soul, that without words, without the necessity of demonstrations of affection, heart beats to heart, soul answers soul, and there is no need of words.

Harriet Beecher Stowe

What is dying?
A ship sails and I stand watching till she fades on the horizon and someone at my side says, 'She is gone.' Gone where? Gone from my sight, that is all; she is just as large as when I saw her. The diminished size, and total loss of sight is in me, not in her, and just at the moment when someone at my side says, 'She is gone,' there are others who are watching her coming, and other voices take up a glad shout, 'There she comes!' and that is dying.

Bishop Brent

The cry of man's anguish went up to God,
'Lord, take away pain!
The shadow that darkens the world thou
    hast made;
The close coiling chain
That strangles the heart: the burden that weighs
On the wings that would soar –
Lord, take away pain from the world thou
    hast made
That it love thee the more!'

Then answered the Lord to the cry of the world,
'Shall I take away pain,
And with it the power of the soul to endure,
Made strong by the strain?
Shall I take away pity that knits heart to heart,
And sacrifice high?
Will ye lose all your heroes that lift from the fire
White brows to the sky?
Shall I take away love that redeems with a price,
And smiles with its loss?
Can ye spare from your lives that would cling
    unto mine
The Christ on his cross?'

Anonymous

Here lies a woman who was always tired,
She lived in a house where help was not hired,
Her last words on earth were: 'Dear friends, I am going
Where washing ain't done, nor sweeping, nor sewing;
But everything there is exact to my wishes;
For where they don't eat, there's no washing of dishes.
I'll be where loud anthems will always be ringing,
But having no voice, I'll be clear of the singing.
Don't mourn for me now, don't mourn for me never –
I'm going to do nothing for ever and ever.'

Anonymous

Benjamin Franklin, printer,
(Like the cover of an old book,
Its contents worn out,
And stripped of its lettering and gilding)
Lies here, food for worms!
Yet the work itself shall not be lost,
For it will, as he believed, appear once more
In a new
And more beautiful edition,
Corrected and amended
By its Author!

Benjamin Franklin
(suggestion for his own epitaph)

Christmas Afterglow

Nichola Jones

Have you managed to survive that time of the year which the media love and which involves being nice to many mere acquaintances and coping with pressure from all sides? Are you worn out now that Christmas is over? No matter how many folk you got to kiss under the mistletoe, or how many presents you received, or how great the party was – when it's all over, don't you feel shattered and exhausted?

And if you've just spent Christmas on your own, or had a row with someone, or are feeling pretty desperate, isn't it ghastly when everyone harps on about Christmas cheer and the season of goodwill? What's left to show after it's all done? A scraggy, weary tree and sagging tinsel, a house looking like the last day of the sales, a fridge full of leftovers, and television full of gruesome repeats.

What do we take with us back to ordinary life as we turn towards the new year? Perhaps some presents which really were what we wanted; perhaps some new friendships or the healing of some broken ones; perhaps photos or videos of family get-togethers which did work out after all.

After the fuss is over, I remember some special things: Christmas Eve and Midnight Communion, and seven-year-old Peter being allowed to stay up as a special treat. He's one of the noisiest children in church, always fidgeting and falling off his seat. He walks down the long aisle, holding his mum's hand and kneels at the front. For a blessing. His little face is radiant, wide-eyed with wonder at the blaze of candles and the beautiful music.

Behind him comes Lucy, so very frail at nearly ninety and showing every year. She doesn't kneel because if she once got down, she would never get up. Lucy stands at the Communion rail and holds out her gnarled, brown hands, freckled and lined, twisted with arthritis, trembling very slightly. She's come on her own. Many of her friends have gone – she's outlived them all – but her face is filled with love and hope.

There's a big commotion at the door and striding down the aisle are four lads from the club across the way. They're part of the darts team and wanted to come to Midnight Mass. They burst in with a blast of cold air and alcoholic fumes. But when they reach the front, they kneel with bowed heads and ask for a prayer to be said for their mate who came off his bike and is in hospital.

Next to them kneels Barry and his teenage daughter Helen, both neatly dressed and well turned out. As you glance at Barry's face, tears are pouring down. Three months ago his wife died from cancer and he doesn't know how to keep going. He's come to church because last year they came here together and he feels close to her tonight. And your heart aches for him and his daughter.

And your heart aches for all those people who haven't known how to keep going. More than any tinsel or decorations, they want to know about Hope. They want to know that this life isn't all there is. That there's a reason to go on living. That God's love and grace reaches out to them now, and in the world to come.

How dare Christians say that?

Because at the heart of Christmas is a tiny little baby, frail and vulnerable, who grows to be a marvellous man, in whom God is most clearly seen, who shakes the world by his teaching and deeds, who dies and conquers death, and is alive today, offering us new life and new hope. (Not only in this life but for the world to come.)

Are you bored with your life? Or worried about the future? Or tired out with it all? Then think on Jesus who says, 'God is with us always. And God loves you utterly and forever.' Now that's a Christmas message worth holding on to!

Long, long, long ago;
Way before this winter's snow
First fell upon these weathered fields;
I used to sit and watch and feel
And dream of how the spring would be,
When through the winter's stormy sea
She'd raise her green and growing head,
Her warmth would resurrect the dead.

Long before this winter's snow
I dreamt of this day's sunny glow
And thought somehow my pain would pass
With winter's pain, and peace like grass
Would simply grow. The pain's not gone.
It's still as cold and hard and long
As lonely pain has ever been,
It cuts so deep and far within.

Long before this winter's snow
I ran from pain, looked high and low
For some fast way to get around
Its hurt and cold. I'd have found,
If I had looked at what was there,
That things don't follow fast or fair.
That life goes on, and times do change,
And grass does grow despite life's pains.

Long before this winter's snow
I thought that this day's sunny glow,
The smiling children and growing things
And flowers bright were brought by spring.
Now, I know the sun does shine,
That children smile, and from the dark, cold, grime
A flower comes. It groans, yet sings,
And through its pain, its peace begins.

Mary Ann Thompson, Resurrection

Death is mysterious, awe-inspiring, and scary. Yet we live in a society today in which people are caught up in the whirlwind of the chase after money, jobs, family and personal cares. Death is not the immediate reality it used to be. Many people just don't want to face death. If you ask most men, but not necessarily women, how they would like to die, most would say they would like to die suddenly and not to know. For myself, I would never choose that. I would choose to have the chance to say 'I'm sorry' and 'thank you', to do a little tidying up.

Dame Cicely Saunders

God, we are as confounded as Joseph and Mary, as busy as the innkeepers, as lonely as the shepherds, as frightened as Herod, as wayfaring as the Magi. Turn us again to the place, where, with quietness, you wrap up your truth and promise in the Child born in a rude stable. We would ponder these things as the noise and clamour of the world is stilled for a time and there is a peace that settles deep within us. Bring us to Bethlehem, to the place where he was homeless, but where we are truly at home.

Donald J. Shelby,
The Unsettling Season

It's been three weeks since you closed the garage door, sat in your '66 Chevy, and started an irreversible process that ended two days later when the Denver coroner called to tell me you were in a hurry to join Mother.

I'm still angry at you.

I know you missed her – we all did. You were good to stand by her during the last ugly stages of her Alzheimer's disease. A weaker person would have sent her to an institution, but you lived with a daily nightmare until she mercifully died.

I'm sorry I did not take you seriously when, at Mother's funeral, you said, 'I have nothing to live for.' I foolishly believed that was grief speaking and not you. Now I know you meant it. But that does not lessen my anger toward you. I said then, and still believe, that you had everything to live for. You had thirteen grandchildren and eight great-grandchildren. You were free of the emotionally draining 24-hour-a-day care of Mother. And you had your health.

I fully understand persons taking their lives when they are in agony and without hope. But you were in no physical pain, and you had the hope that the emotional pain of Mother's death would ease with time.

I'm sure that if I am right – that taking your life was wrong – that God has long since forgiven that act. He has embraced you with his love. I'm equally sure that as time passes, I too will forgive you. Feelings of hurt and anger will be replaced by memories of better times.

But for now my memories are only of a soot-filled garage that obliterates all happy boyhood memories. I feel robbed of normal grief.

We are entering the Advent season, a time when we prepare ourselves for the coming of the Christ child. Everything will seem different this year, Dad. Somehow the coming of Christ – a Christ who will forgive, renew and promise eternal life – goes beyond sentimentality this year. As he forgives you and as he takes you and Mother into his care, I pray that I too will learn to forgive you, and to provide extra helpings of love and support for those you've left behind.

J. Richard Peck

When I am dead
Cry for me a little
Think of me sometimes
But not too much.
Think of me now and again
As I was in life
At some moments it's pleasant
*   to recall*
But not for long.
Leave me in peace
And I shall leave you in peace
And while you live
Let your thoughts be with the living.

Indian prayer

On Thinking about Being Old

Donald Soper

'Youth looks forward. Age looks backward' is all very well as a proposition for a debate, but in itself it is a dangerous cliché. Nevertheless it is one way, however imperfect, of describing the 'shift of attention' that is characteristic in old people. I tend to 'dwell' in the past precisely because I can only 'squat' in the future.

Increasingly memory becomes the preoccupation of the mind of the elderly; but I have by no means found it an unmitigated blessing. There is nothing automatically pleasurable in remembering the past. Such a recovery of what has gone before contains much to be ashamed of, much to regret, and so many breaks in anything that could be called a chain of events. No one who remembers the past can recall it with the impartiality of a computer. Human beings are never impartial, however hard they try to subjugate their personal prejudices to the demand of objectivity. The mind of man is incurably and constitutionally selective.

As an old man, I am always on the look out for happiness, and so I eagerly recapture past experiences which on recollection give me pleasure. In that respect memory is episodic rather than continuous. Holidays as I remember them were always sunlit: looking back it never seemed to rain in Minehead during August when I was a boy. On the other hand I have a love-hate relationship with my memories and find comfort, as I am convinced others do, in the deliberate recall of painful matters, disasters of one kind or another, mistreatment by those who failed (as I imagined) to understand me, et cetera. My first infant romance, the unrequited affection I offered to my sister's girlfriend – how I suffered! – and how it lives and thrives in my memory. There is a kind of gruesome satisfaction to bringing to mind the miseries as well as the joys of yesteryear. Often we can wallow in them – why not?

This recall of things that would otherwise remain forgotten can give a sort of dignity to the ageing process. It establishes the 'me' of my memories with a sense of continuity and significance. It is finding myself as a person rather than a succession of unrelated episodes. It is not simplistic to say that what many old people most need is to feel that they are 'somebody' not 'anybody'. This kind of permanent identity can accompany memory in old age. Marcel Proust in his saga about the quest and rehabilitation of the past (A la recherche du temps perdu) believes this is especially related to art and poetry and music. In his vast book Proust finds in the world of imagination and beauty meaning that can – to misquote Shakespeare – 'knit up the ravelled sleeve of our memories'.

I wonder how many old people, through no fault of their own, fail to find the kind of blessing that the world of poetry, imagination and music can offer. It requires a diligent apprenticeship and I have found it infinitely worthwhile.

Here is a quotation that belongs to my religious experience. It is the 'royalty of inward happiness that comes from living close to God'. I commend a companion truth. There is also the royalty of inward happiness in coming close to the world of imagination and art, and every time we choose to enter that world in recollection, if not in prospect, we are the better for that excursion. After all, surely the world of Christian belief is the same world of music and poetry and beauty.

Another predominant accompaniment of age is, in my experience, restrictions of various kinds. I can't get about because my legs won't let me. I can't read for long because my eyes won't let me. I can't hear a conversation, and people think I'm not listening properly. I can't talk as once I did to other people because to quote the hymn – 'my company is gone before'. I feel 'shrivelled' like the lines on my face, as if a kind of lifelessness has happened to me. Of course, it need not be as bad as all that but it promotes a kind of loneliness. I don't seem to 'belong' as once I did.

Religion for me is the belief in, and experience of, one fundamental answer to this condition of separation. We are not 'out on our own' but are members one of another, whether in the Christian concept of God's family, or the Pantheistic Buddhist concept of absorption. Because our immediate experience does not look like that, the beginning of this religious journey must be some kind of leap in the dark. It is what is called a venture of faith, and I can vouch for its effectiveness. The more I have cultivated this good news of 'belonging' the more satisfying it has become.

It is more than a compensation for the restrictions of old age. It is the sort of peace which passes understanding but it is real and lasting for all that. In principle the elderly need the living fellowship of corporate Christianity, ie. the Church. This fellowship of believers can provide a kind of fulfilment which takes the place of the restriction of old age. Organised religion can make old and lonely human beings feel at home as a recovery of a transient past, or the first intimation of a welcoming future.

I share, as an old man, the feeling which other old people have also expressed to me, that those who are not elderly don't appear to try nearly hard enough to understand what it is like to be getting 'past it'. Caring for elderly people demands an intimate sympathy for something which in youth is little more than a statistic. One of the dominant thoughts that occupy the mind is the contemplation of a future identified with death. There is significance in Dr Johnson's claim that a sentence of death marvellously concentrates the mind. Youth can postpone such a concentration. Age is increasingly aware of its universal and approaching inevitability.

I will presume to write something about this sentence of death which is ever present, and is only too obsessive. I write as a would-be Christian, but start with a caveat. I firmly believe in what Jesus called eternal life, though I hasten to add that I don't know very much about it. Moreover I become increasingly suspicious of those who seem to know more about the nature and meaning of life beyond death than they do about everyday affairs down here.

To begin with, I can only come to terms with the problems of the future if I possess the necessary instruments for undertaking such a task. The plain fact is that neither I nor anybody else has that complete set of tools. Out of my own experience I would counsel the reader to be very wary of so-called information from the 'other side'. I understand those who crave for the sound of 'departed voices', or the message transmitted by those who claim to receive direct messages from the other side. I have attended seances and read diligently in this field. I have never found it revelatory. Without impugning the intended sincerity of the medium I do not believe these experiences testify to the 'celestial mansions'. They are at best excursions 'round the houses' down here.

This does not mean that the pervading contemplation of death sooner or later is a waste of time or an incurable melancholy. If in one sense I cannot believe in a worthwhile life after death, as I can believe in a sunrise tomorrow morning, I find it profoundly significant that I should want to believe in it. Why should I want to be reunited with loved ones? Why should I want to continue to have some sort of knowledge or contact with those I leave behind when I die? My personal conviction, that deepens with my length of days, is that we are made that way, made for God, and therefore we are restless till we rest in his eternity. I can't prove such an assumption but I can reasonably hope for it.

As an old man, I am satisfied that this cultivation of hope is a healing process, and that it is found in the middle of faith and love, as St Paul says. There are impediments to faith. There are peaks of love which in all honesty we know we cannot climb, but there is no bar to hope. To say that I will hope in the face of apparent contradiction is an infinitely worthwhile determination. Arguments about death can stop us in our tracks, but nothing can prevent me from deciding that I will go on hoping. This is the supreme blessing. It can give the elderly like me the wages of going on 'when faith grows dim' and love seems hard to find.

As a minister of the Christian gospel I have found the occasion and stimulation of hope in the regular practice of prayer and worship; and perhaps even more in the congregation of hope – the corporate proclamation that God's kingdom is coming, and whenever and wherever it comes, we must be prepared to be members of it.

The immortal Blaise Pascal offered to the aged a wager infinitely worth making. Believe in the life of heaven beyond death. If it comes off, you win. If you lose, it won't matter because you won't know you've lost; but isn't that realisation the beginning of eternal life?

Those who live in the Lord never see each other for the last time.

German proverb

Warned from the body to depart,
What shall I of my God desire?
Pardon and grace to keep my heart
Till thou my ready soul require.

All that is past, my God, forgive;
For the short time to come defend;
And strengthening without sin to live,
Oh bless me with a peaceful end.

Meet for the fellowship above,
The glories of eternity,
Thy servant, Lord, with ease remove,
And let me fall asleep in thee.

Do thou, if so thy love ordain,
Gently the knot of life untie;
And free from sin, and free from pain,
In mercy's arms I sweetly die.

Charles Wesley

When a man dies he clutches in his hands only that which he has given away in his lifetime.

Jean Jacques Rousseau

Would Mark miss us as much as we would miss him? I am confident that the joy of being with his heavenly Father more than compensates for the absence of earthly parents and am comforted by the thought that God's time is not our time and it will seem no time at all to Mark until we are united. Also, as friends sought to find appropriate words during those first few hours an oft repeated phrase was 'he's running around in heaven now'. Yes, imagine his joy at being freed from that restricting body, free to dance, free to run!

What other than joy could there be for a little boy for whom Jesus had been so important? How he loved Jesus! How precious those 'Jesus books' were! His joy in sharing in the communion service, his delight in the story of the risen Lord leading to his hope of being united forever with Jesus in heaven. How hard we had prayed that Mark be physically cured! That was not to be, but he became whole spiritually. In losing his life he has found the joy of eternal life in Jesus.

Mary Austin, *Free to Dance with the Lord of the Dance*

Here at Stoke-by-Nayland once lived a wealthy miser who pulled down crows' nests for fuel and got the usual reward of such-like thrift in having half-a-million of money half-a-minute before he died, and nothing half-a-minute later.

Epitaph

Good Friday

O heart, be lifted up; O heart be gay,
Because the Light was lifted up today —
Was lifted on the Rood, but did not die,
To shine eternally for such as I.

O heart, rejoice with all your humble might
That God did kindle in the world this Light,
Which stretching on the Cross could not prevent
From shining with continuous intent.

Why weep, O heart, this day? Why grieve you so?
If all the glory of the Light had lost its glow
Would the sun shine or earth put on her best —
Her flower-entangled and embroidered vest?

Look up, O heart; and then, O heart, kneel down
In humble adoration: give no crown
Nor golden diadem to your fair Lord,
But offer love and beauty by your word.

Let your faith burn, O heart: and let your eyes
Shine with such joy where deepest night still lies
In some too tired and over-burdened mind:
Let Christ be seen, wherever you are kind.

O heart, let your light shine so that all men
May see your works and glorify again
Your Father: and oh! let your light be gay,
And full of quiet laughter all the day.

The everlasting fire of love, O heart,
Has blazed in you and it will not depart.
Wherefore, O heart, exult and praises sing:
Lift up your voice and make the echoes ring.

Raise up your hands, O heart: your fingers raise
In adoration; and in bursting praise
Sing all your songs of beauty with delight,
You larks, exulting in the summer light.

O heart, rise up: O heart be lifted high.
Rejoice; for Light was slain today, yet did not die.

Anonymous

But in the night of death, hope sees a star and listening love can hear the rustling of a wing.

Author unknown

Grief knits two hearts in closer bonds than happiness ever can, and common suffering is a far stronger link than common joy.

Alphonse De Lamartine

Jesus died to square a circle. A holy God and yet a Saviour is a paradox, if not an outright contradiction. A saviour God calls you to him; a holy God has no option but to condemn you for your sinfulness when you get there. He can't just wipe the slate clean and say, 'Forget it!', for it is on his integrity, his self-consistency that the moral order of the universe depends; without it there would be chaos.

So sin must be paid for. God's holiness has to be upheld. Who could pay the price for the totality of human sinfulness? Certainly not even a Galilean carpenter, however holy and good, called Jesus. Only God has the resources to pay that price. It's a mystery and I don't pretend to understand the nature of the cosmic transaction which took place on Calvary, but the united testimony of the Christian church is that in the suffering and death of Jesus God himself was present. He himself paid the price of sin.

Colin Morris,
Starting from Scratch

Old Age

Michael Hare-Duke

In this world nothing can be said to be certain, except death and taxes. The only questions are 'when' and 'how much?'

The essential realism of that quotation from Benjamin Franklin makes clear the universality of death and with it the process of growing old which leads towards it. By contrast a great deal of our contemporary culture seems dedicated to avoiding the facts. 'Never say die' is a misguided aphorism which encourages denial. Inevitably we are going to die, and as well as asking 'when?' we need to be interested in 'how?', which takes us into a concern about old age.

Of course, it is right to live life to the full and encourage others to do the same, but not in a play-acting denial of the diminishments experienced in old age. For if we deny what is true about ourselves, at that point we will forfeit the opportunity of making an authentic contribution from the genuine gifts that old age brings. Instead we will be adding to the notion that it is something fearful, to be disguised, not owned and celebrated. Moreover Erik Erikson, in his major work *Childhood and Society*, suggests that where death is not handled realistically there is something amiss with the whole structure. He summed this up when he wrote:

> Healthy children will not fear life if their
> elders have integrity enough not to fear death.

Those who deny it, or pretend that they are as young
as they ever were, join those pathetic groups of teenage
geriatrics, in places like California, bopping away on
their Zimmers. Some may collude with the pretence
and say, 'Aren't they marvellous?', but realism asks,
'What has happened to their maturity?' Has life taught
them nothing about a grown-up way of handling loss
so that they do not have to deny the physical truth of
stiffening limbs, the failing memory, the slowing down
of mental agility? There was once an unhealthy play-
acting which took our grandmothers into old age and
black bombazine far too young, but it is a pity if, in
revulsion from this, our generation hoists their mini-
skirts above their varicose veins. As with every stage
of life the need is to find who we are and live at ease
with the truth of ourselves. Perhaps this is the
fundamental gift of old age: to live without the need to
conform to others' images, to dance to nobody's tune
but our own. In doing this the elders might
demonstrate their ultimate lesson, that every
generation should find its own autonomy and live with
a confidence in itself.

In old age, such liberation can derive from the fact that
one is no longer climbing the mountain of ambition,
trying to display abilities beyond one's capacity.
Instead there opens out the possibility of a plateau of
truth: 'This is me, and I am glad to be that way.' That
is easier said than done, because we are brought back
to the fact that old age is the beginning of the dying
process in which we experience the closing down of

options. Up to a certain point in life it is possible to
believe that something new and different is round the
corner; the job that will make up for the
disappointments, the sudden success that will redeem
all the failures; in today's culture there can be the hope
of another, more enriching marriage. Perhaps the
appeal of the National Lottery is that it seems to offer
the otherwise unattainable dream of wealth and
luxury. Without such dreams does life lose its
meaning? Was it a cheat, or have we failed?

One way of dealing with these fears is to turn from the
future and concentrate on the past, to look back to
what might have been. We can imagine ourselves
doing so much better if we had the chance over again.
The career would be differently shaped; family life
lived with space for the things that mattered; sexual
experiences that had only been seen in fiction would be
realised for ourselves; time would be spent in richer
pursuits.

In the Tibetan *Book of the Dead* it is expected that the
person approaching death will be assaulted by such
'hungry ghosts' – all the 'if onlys' which eat away at
the solid achievements which are there to be
celebrated.

But a catalogue of missed opportunities or mistaken
judgements makes it difficult to accept 'Sister Death' as
a friend who opens the way to a new life. All the
attention is focused on the past, leaving the recall of
failure and the negative connotations predominant.
For this reason there is a sensitivity about what
language we should use to describe the old.

Sometimes they are called 'Senior Citizens', or members of 'the Third Age'. In the business world people are designated 'consultants' to save them the indignity or the tax difficulties of retirement. 'Elderly' is preferred to 'old'. We try to get over the problem by a joke and so have coined the names 'wrinklies' or 'crumblies'. By these various shifts of language we are trying to avoid facing the stark truth spelt out by the melancholy Jaques in Shakespeare's *As You Like It*:

And so from hour to hour we ripe and ripe,
and then from hour to hour we rot and rot.

Contemporary society carries equally unacceptable expectations of old age, sometimes exacerbated by the fact that people are, in general, living longer. Geriatric medicine offers renewed mobility through joint replacements; impaired sight and hearing can be greatly improved by artificial aids. Physical medicine overcomes the pneumonia which carried off many of the elderly in winter time and was consequently known as 'the old man's friend'. Medicine has become the victim of its own success. Desperate relatives, caring for an Alzheimer's sufferer or someone similarly disabled, may long for nature to take its course. Consequently the whole debate about living wills and voluntary euthanasia troubles the world of medical ethics. Now that the 'old old', people surviving into their mid-eighties, are a significant demographic feature, there is almost a note of panic as health and social work administrators do their sums and project unsustainable costs in their budgets. Nobody is looking to the contribution which this age-group might be encouraged to make to society at large and their own welfare in particular.

The elderly themselves begin to feel a loss of value and status in society. Unlike the elders of the tribe in a more primitive culture, they do not appear as a resource, guarding a tradition that is important for survival or contributing from their store of remembered experience. 'Old-fashioned' is a term of opprobrium; in a state of rapidly advancing technology, the elderly are left unable to cope with the instructions on the video-recorder, the complexities of the computer or even the conversion to metrification. They feel marginalised, identified with other disadvantaged groups, the victims of 'ageism'.

In civilised societies, dominance does not depend on physical or sexual prowess as in the animal kingdom. Beyond these are wisdom and stored experience and the gifts of love and forgiveness developed over long years. In Russia, as a post-Communist society is seeking to restore the spiritual values of Orthodoxy, it was said, 'Only the grandmothers will know.' With that judgement a whole generation of faithful babuskas came into their own!

In the Psalms one phrase captures this theme:

I am become like a bottle in the smoke.

The image is of a leather wineskin hanging by the fire. The outer surface catches the smoke and hardens, losing the fresh appearance, but within a vintage is maturing, its quality guaranteed by the gnarled outside. Can the human process of maturing acquire and sustain a similar positive view of the individual? Part of our care of the old will need to draw on past wisdom and other cultures to discover how best we can make creative the increasingly long years that are likely to be offered in retirement.

Again it is the Psalmist who offers a hopeful picture:

> Those who are planted in the house of the Lord:
> shall flourish in the courts of our God.
>
> They shall still bear fruit in old age;
> they shall be green and succulent.

(Psalm 92: 12,13)

Two elements are required for a renewed spiritual care of the elderly. First there is needed a coherent body of thought and practice which offers a way of handling the daily experience of growing old and accepting the inevitability of death. Alongside the theory is required a body of mature believers who can act as guides to others who are consciously embarked on this process.

There are resources in the great world religions which helpfully complement each other. The Buddhists have set out a path in their teaching about death as a transition or 'bardo' process. One primary source, already quoted, is the Tibetan *Book of the Dead*, documenting the stages as they have perceived them. The teaching amplified in later writings is almost a guide book to the country that stretches this side of death and beyond it.

Within the Christian Churches there has also been a long history of helping people along this path. We share with Judaism the profound heritage of the Psalms which build up confidence in the history of God's dealing with his people, corporately and individually. This faith offers a context in which life can be lived with an assurance of ultimate care and goodwill, however tragic or painful the present may be.

The uniquely Christian contribution is the pattern of life out of death that is rooted in the faith of the resurrection of Jesus. It has issued in such classical expressions as Bunyan's *Pilgrim's Progress*. More importantly the practice of accompanying individuals on their journey of faith has developed especially from the tradition of Ignatian spirituality and has much to contribute to the development of faith in eternal life.

This is not a remote hope but a reality already experienced in the ordinary course of human life. Each stage has about it an element of loss and discovery, death and new life. To be born requires the foetus to lose the security of the womb and accept expulsion into the frightening outer world. Throughout childhood, this is followed by the processes of growth that in their turn feel like little deaths, as when the child moves from the comfort of the family circle into the wider world of school with its potentially threatening demands. This then develops into a safe environment, with a trusted group of friends whom we later fear to lose in the next stage of growth. Successfully transcending each of these crises can lead us into a confidence that the pattern of recovery out of loss can be trusted to hold, even in the ultimate experience of death.

There is an explicit task to be undertaken of clarifying and bringing together these various perceptions so that they provide a kind of map. We need to collect the images of death that so many traditions enshrine. In this way what has come to be experienced as the diminishment of old age can be redefined as the unbinding of a person's attachments to objects that need to be outgrown and then he or she can be sent on their way, not in isolation but with a new sense of accompaniment which is enshrined in the old prayer that has been recently reminted:

> Go forth upon your journey from this world,
> dear child of God,
> into the hands of the Father who made you,
> to find life in Christ who redeemed you,
> to rejoice in the Spirit who renews you.
> May the heavenly host sustain you
> and the company of the redeemed enfold you;
> may peace be yours this day, and the heavenly
> city your home.

In that is encapsulated the message that death is neither isolating nor destructive; the images are of movement, welcome and purpose and in this is also the opposite of the fears we have about old age itself. The two go together and it is a religious dimension, worked out in a practical spirituality which can bring to them the rainbow image of a positive future.

Celebrate the Third Age:

> Those who are planted in the house of the Lord,
> shall flourish in the courts of our God.
> They shall still bear fruit in old age,
> they shall be green and succulent.

(Psalm 92: 12, 13)

I've seen withered roots, clawing on to life
in soured soil;
spindly branches, brittle with frustration,
ready to crackle when anger strikes.
This is the desert of the unfertile intelligence,
swept by the bitter music of the piper
for whom nobody danced.
Half liberator, jackal Death
waits to crunch the carcass, dried to an untimely end
by disappointment.

Jewels of fruit glisten on other trees
that tap into deep reservoirs of being.
Watered by affection, they blossom
in the spring time of maturity.
At home in the delight of God
they express the green glory of creation;
to the last, the sap rises
and laughter stirs in the supple leaves.

M. H-D.

If some king of the earth have so large an extent of dominion in north and south as that he hath winter and summer together in his dominions, so large an extent east and west as that he hath day and night together in his dominions, much more hath God mercy and judgement together. He brought light out of darkness, not out of a lesser light. He can bring thy summer out of winter though thou have no spring. Though in the ways of fortune, or misunderstanding, or conscience, thou have been benighted till now, wintred and frozen, clouded and eclipsed, damp and benumbed, smothered and stupified till now, now God comes to thee, not as in the dawning of the day, not as in the bud of the spring, but as the sun at noon, to banish all shadows; as the sheaves in harvest, to fill all penuries. All occasions invite his mercies, and all times are his seasons.

John Donne

Contributors

Eddie Askew and his wife, Barbara, served in India for fifteen years with the Leprosy Mission. He later became its International Director. Now retired, he is a best-selling Christian author whose books have sold half a million copies. He exhibits regularly as an artist, and is actively involved in the National Retreat Movement.

Hazel Bradley is a teacher of Religious Studies, a freelance producer of religious programmes for BBC Radio Merseyside, and has written two books, *Hazel's Hymns* and *More Hazel's Hymns* about the origins and history of well-known hymns. She is married with two children, and is a local preacher in the Warrington circuit of the Methodist Church.

Rev David Coffey trained at Spurgeon's College and has especial expertise in mission, evangelism and worship. He has ministered at pastorates in Leicestershire, Surrey and Devon, and has held various posts in the Baptist Union of Great Britain: President (1986-87), Head of the Mission Department (1988-91) and General Secretary since 1991. He has also been Vice-President of the European Baptist Federation, and in 1997 will become its President.

SEASONS OF LIFE

Baroness Cox says she is a nurse and social scientist by intention and a politician by surprise, having been appointed a Life Peer in 1982. She now spends much of her time with Christian Solidarity International (CSI), an inter-church organisation working for victims of repression, regardless of colour, creed or nationality. She is also Chancellor of Bournemouth University, serves on the Board of the Teacher Training Agency, is a Vice-President of the Royal College of Nursing and President of CSI-UK.

Rev Dr Stephen Dawes is a Methodist minister who has served in the circuits of Hexham, Stafford and Bodmin. He has also worked in theological colleges in Ghana and Birmingham (as Old Testament tutor at Queen's College). He is now the Chairman of the Cornwall District of the Methodist Church.

Rt Rev Timothy Dudley-Smith retired in 1991 after almost twenty years in the Diocese of Norwich, as Archdeacon of Norwich and then as Bishop of Thetford. He has been writing hymn texts for more than thirty years, usually on holiday in Cornwall during August, and still aims to write six or eight new texts a year. His collected texts now number about two hundred, and his three collections of texts are *Lift Every Heart* (1984), *Songs of Deliverance* (1988) and *A Voice of Singing* (1993).

Andrew Dyer is the son of a Methodist minister. At the time of writing his contribution to *Seasons of Life* he was in his final year at the University of Brighton, and has since attained a B.A. (Hons) degree in Accounting and Finance. In July 1996 he began work as a Finance Officer at the University of Hertfordshire in Hatfield.

Rev Dr Leslie Griffiths has been a Methodist minister since 1968. The first four years of his ministry were spent in Haiti and he later returned there for a further three years. He has also served in Reading, and as Superintendent of the Finchley and Hendon circuit. He was President of the Methodist Conference 1994-95, and in September 1996 he was appointed Superintendent of Wesley's Chapel-Leysian Centre in London. He writes a monthly column for the *Methodist Recorder*.

Rt Rev Michael Hare-Duke was ordained in 1952 and served as a parish priest in London, Lancashire and Nottingham. He was the first Pastoral Director of the Clinical Theology Association. In 1969 he was appointed Bishop of St Andrews, retiring in 1994. Currently Chairman of Age Concern, Scotland, he is the author of a number of books, which include *Stories, Signs and Sacraments of the Emerging Church* (1982), *Praying for Peace, reflections on the Gulf Crisis* (1991) and *Hearing the Stranger* (1994).

Rev Nichola Jones, a Methodist minister for fourteen years, serves two churches in Bloxwich and Walsall. As a teenager, growing up as a minister's daughter, she felt Christ calling her into the ministry. She enjoys meeting all sorts of people, celebrating God in worship, and serving Christ in the community.

Philip Jones works for the Methodist Publishing House and is a local preacher. His background is in bookselling and he has previously undertaken pastoral work for the Methodist Church. He is married with two children.

Bruce Kent is a retired Roman Catholic priest, now married. He has had a variety of pastoral responsibilities, ranging from university chaplain to parish priest. Most of his life has been spent working with peace and justice organisations. They range from the United Nations Association and Pax Christi to CND and the Campaign Against the Arms Trade.

Rev Dr John Newton is a Methodist minister who has served in the circuits of Louth, Stockton-on-Tees and the West London Mission. He taught theology and church history at Richmond College, Wesley College, Bristol, and St Paul's College, Limuru, Kenya. Recently he retired from the chairmanship of the Liverpool District, and is at present Warden of John Wesley's Chapel, the New Room, Bristol. He is married and has four sons.

Rev Ann Shepherdson has served as a deaconess in the Midlands, Yorkshire and the north east. As a Methodist minister she has worked in Tyne and Wear and is now based in Bath. She is the author of *Comfort for the Journey Home*, a series of meditations for the terminally ill, and is also a director of the *Methodist Recorder*.

Rev The Lord Soper entered the Methodist ministry in 1926, and served for forty-two years as Superintendent of the West London Mission. He was President of the Methodist Conference 1953-54 and was created a Life Peer in 1965. He has spoken in the open air for seventy years.

Rev Frank Topping is a Methodist minister who works in broadcasting and the theatre. A prolific writer, he has written thousands of scripts for BBC Radio, several TV series and fourteen books. He is a songwriter, a prize-winning playwright and also an actor, who has appeared in the West End.

Deacon Les Wallace is a member of the Methodist Diaconal Order and was stationed in Dogsthorpe, Peterborough in 1994, after initial training at Wesley House, Cambridge, and circuit work in South Norfolk. He is married and has two children.

Lord Weatherill was MP for Croydon NE from 1964-92 and Speaker of the House of Commons from 1983-92. Throughout this period he was an active member of he Parliamentary Christian Fellowship. In the House of Lords he is Convenor of the Cross Bench (Independent) Peers. An Anglican – he is High Baliff of Westminster Abbey – he is also Patron of Wesley's Chapel, and therefore can claim to be an honorary Methodist!

Dr Pauline Webb is a Methodist local preacher and a former Vice-President of the Methodist Conference. She has worked with the Methodist Overseas Division as Editor and later as Organiser of Religious Broadcasting with the BBC World Service. Now retired, she is still active as a freelance broadcaster and writer.

Rev Brenda Woods spent twenty-five years teaching mainly Physics in a comprehensive school in London, with three years at Waddilove, a Methodist mission school in Zimbabwe. Now a Methodist minister in the Peterborough circuit, she has a particular interest in spirituality and in enabling people to deepen their faith through working together in small groups.

Acknowledgements

Methodist Publishing House gratefully acknowledges permission to use copyright items. Every effort has been made to trace copyright owners, but where we have been unsuccessful we would welcome information which would enable us to make appropriate acknowledgement in any reprint.

The extract from *Disguises of Love* by Eddie Askew is reproduced by permission of The Leprosy Mission, Goldhay Way, Orton Goldhay, Peterborough, PE2 5GZ.

'Youth: Living, Dying and Asking: 'Dear God – why?' by Frank Topping is an extract from Frank Topping's autobiography, *Laughing in my Sleep,* published 1993 and reproduced by permission of Hodder & Stoughton Limited.

Scripture quotations, unless otherwise stated, are from the New Revised Standard Version of the Bible, copyright 1989 by the Division of Christian Education of the National Council of the Churches of Christ in the USA.

Page

11   Rupert E. Davies, *Methodism,* Epworth Press.

19   'An Interview with Bishop Trevor Huddleston, Apartheid's Veteran Opponent', *International Christian Digest*, February 1988.

28   Avery Brooke, from *Weavings: A Journal of the Christian Spiritual Life*, Vol V, No 2. Copyright 1990 by The Upper Room, Nashville, Tennessee. Used by permission.

28   David Deeks, *Pastoral Theology: An Inquiry*, Epworth Press.

29   'Frances Young: Author, Preacher, Professor, Supermum', *International Christian Digest*, May 1988.

30   Michael E. Williams, from *Weavings: A Journal of the Christian Spiritual Life*, vol. V, No. 4. Copyright 1990 by The Upper Room, Nashville, Tennessee. Used by permission.

38   Leslie Church, *The Homely Year*, Epworth Press.

39   A. G. Ives, *'Kingswood School in Wesley's Day and Since'*, Epworth Press.

39   Gordon Wakefield, *Methodist Devotion*, Epworth Press.

41   J. B. Phillips, *Your God is too Small*, Epworth Press.

42   John Killinger, from *Beginning Prayer*, Copyright © 1993 by John Killinger. Used by permission of The Upper Room.

51   Leslie D. Weatherhead, *Jesus and Ourselves*, Epworth Press.

82 Richard P. Heitzenrater, 'Wesley and his Diary', *John Wesley: Contemporary Perspectives*, ed. John Stacey, Epworth Press.

95 Michael McMullen ed. *Hearts Aflame*, Triangle/SPCK.

123 Richard Adams, *Visions and Voices*, Epworth Press.

125 Patricia Wilson, from *How Can I Be Over the Hill When I Haven't Seen the Top Yet?* Copyright © 1989 by Patricia Wilson. Used by permission of The Upper Room.

133 Fairfields Whitwell, *The Hill of Contentment*, Epworth Press.

136 Katherine Price Hughes, *The Story of My Life*, Epworth Press.

147 Maxie Dunnam, from *Jesus' Claims – Our Promises*, Copyright © 1985 by The Upper Room. Used by permission of the publisher.

164 'Resurrection', Mary Ann Thompson. Used by permission.

165 'Dame Cicely Saunders, Founder of the Hospice Movement', *International Christian Digest*, April 1988.

165 Donald J. Shelby, from *The Unsettling Season*, Copyright © 1989 by Donald J. Shelby. Used by permission of The Upper Room

167   J. Richard Peck, Editorial, *International Christian Digest*, November 1988.

175   Mary Austin, *Free to Dance with the Lord of the Dance*, Epworth Press.

178   Colin Morris, *Starting from Scratch*, Epworth Press.